Churches of
the New Testament

Ethan R. Longhenry

Churches of the New Testament
© 2008 by DeWard Publishing Company, Ltd.
P.O. Box 6259, Chillicothe, Ohio 45601
800.300.9778
www.dewardpublishing.com

Unless otherwise noted, all scripture quotations are taken from the American Standard Version of the Bible.

Reasonable care has been taken to trace original sources for any excerpts and quotations appearing in this book and to document such information. For material not the public domain, fair-use standards and practices were followed. Should any attribution be found to be incorrect or incomplete, the publisher welcomes written documentation supporting correction for subsequent printings.

Printed in the United States of America.

ISBN: 978-0-9798893-6-3

Acknowledgements

Few endeavors are possible without the encouragement and support of others, and this work is no exception. I would first like to thank God, without whom none of this would be possible; Christ, for His sacrifice and building of His church; and the Holy Spirit, without whose revelation this study would not exist.

I would also like to thank the brethren of the church of Christ in Norwalk, Ohio, who patiently endured a series of lessons on these subjects. Special thanks go to Matt Hennecke and Philip Chumbley and their Manna Bible Maps for graciously allowing their material to be published in this work. Thank you also to DeWard Publishing for all their effort in getting this study to the presses.

I am greatly indebted to my wife and copy editor, Sarah, and my children, Julianna, Maia, and Nathaniel, for encouraging me throughout the process and for suffering the loss of time with me while I researched and wrote the study.

I pray that this study is a benefit to your understanding of God's will and an encouragement to you in your faith.

Notes

Dates are given according to the Before the Common Era (BCE) and Common Era (CE) format. The dates are identical to Before Christ (BC) and In the Year of our Lord/*Anno Domini* (AD) format. I've chosen to use this format because the traditional format is inaccurate (Jesus was born in 4 BCE, and the Kingdom was not inaugurated until 30 CE), Jesus never commanded such a thing, and the system comes from the sixth century CE, not the New Testament.

Reference to early Christian literature or secondary sources does not imply belief in inspiration of these sources or that they are authoritative in any way. They are presented as historical witnesses to the situation of the churches in the period immediately after the New Testament.

If you desire to contact me regarding anything presented in this study, feel free to do so **deusvitae@hotmail.com**.

Contents

Introduction

"And I also say unto thee, that thou art Peter, and upon this rock I will build my church; and the gates of Hades shall not prevail against it." (Matt 16.18)

As soon as the disciples had indicated that they understood that Jesus of Nazareth was the Christ, the Son of the Living God, Jesus spoke of the church that He would build. The church had always been part of God's plan (*cf.* Eph 3.11), and in His wisdom, God established both the universal body of believers in His Son (*cf.* Eph 5.22–33) and also local churches, some form of a manifestation of the universal body in a particular area (*cf.* 1 Cor 1.1–2, Phil 1.1, *etc.*).

These events all occurred well over 1,900 years ago. All of the people mentioned in the New Testament, save Jesus Himself, are long dead and buried. We live in a different time period in a different place and culture with a different language and different technologies. Nevertheless, we believe that the church remains, according to the promise of God (*cf.* Matt 28.18–20). The same message preached to the Mediterranean world of the first century is to be preached in the twenty-first century (*cf.* Gal 1.6–9).

But what is to be done about the church? We live in a world with many different views about the church and what it ought to be. Many in denominations believe more or less in a tradition—the church has changed in many ways over the intervening millennia. Such is acceptable and even welcomed. To many, differences in emphasis, teaching, and practice between what was recorded in the first century and today do not matter. Changes that have become traditions receive as many—if not more—"votes" than what the New Testament records in terms of what is believed and practiced. Many others feel that the church must conform to its environment; the New Testament is interesting history, but only as a witness to events.

Nevertheless, the Bible itself would claim much more than this. Paul declares that any other teaching than the one to which he committed to the believers is *anathema,* or accursed (Gal 1.6–9). The Scriptures bear the promise that they are sufficient "for every good work" (*cf.* 2 Tim 3.16–17). There are many who take this promise seriously, and they desire to represent the New Testament church as much as possible.

As Christians, we ought to believe that God has not left us with no bearings in the twenty-first century, and should therefore look to His inspired Word for direction (Col 3.17). We seek to live by Christ's authority, and to do so, we must find the authority within His word! As this is true of the individual, so also it ought to be with the church. But how can we go about this? How can we establish what the New Testament church represents? Such is the purpose of our study: an investigation of the churches in the New Testament that will establish what God desires—and does not desire—from local churches of Christ.

The Right Path?

Is this a profitable study? Is this the type of study that will indeed help local churches to be more pleasing to God? There are many who have heard an oversimplified version of the appeal to be the "New Testament church" and have criticized even the concept— why would you want to be the New Testament church when so many of those churches were fraught with problems? How can you be a first century church in the twenty-first century? These are important questions to consider, and we must make sure that we understand what we are and are not trying to do.

The endeavor of striving to be the New Testament church is not an attempt to make a facsimile of what we see in the New Testament. No one thinks that we ought to wear togas, speak in Greek, meet in Roman-style homes, or other such things to become the "New Testament church." Neither does anyone think that we ought to follow in the beliefs and practices in those churches condemned by the apostles.

Attempting to be as the New Testament church derives from a conviction regarding the value of Biblical examples. It is universally accepted within all "Christendom" that the Scriptures represent the highest form of authority for Christians today; many also believe that it is the only source of authority for Christian life and practice. Those who strive to be as the first century church believe that the Scriptures are the only source of authority present today for Christian life and practice, and therefore when Christians build upon the Scriptures, they build on firm ground. If it can be known that God commended, say, Antioch in their fervor for evangelism and mission, or the churches in Macedonia for their generosity to the saints, then when Christians today strive to have fervor for evangelism and mission in a local church today, or when a local church is generous to the saints, they will receive the same commendation. Therefore, we should seek to follow the approved examples of the churches of the New Testament today so that we may be similarly approved by God (*cf.* 1 Cor 11.1). Is this confidence in example valid?

The Power of Example

The idea of using Biblical example as authoritative and binding is not popular in many circles of Christianity. While it must be recognized that not every example is binding, that examples are sometimes "contradictory" and thus demonstrate the presence of liberties in action, such should not deter us from considering the value and power of examples. Examples help us make sense of what God has commanded and provide a powerful display of the faith in action.

For instance, Jesus commanded in Matthew 5.44 to love your enemies and to pray for those who persecute you. This is well and good; we can understand this command in the abstract and can consider many ways in which we could put it into practice. Nevertheless, we see that when Jesus was being crucified, He prayed to God that He might "forgive them, for they know not what they do" (Luke 23.34). It is one thing to say to love your enemies; it is far more powerful to see Jesus doing that very thing in the midst of such suffering, anguish, hostility, and hatred. The lesson is clear: if Jesus could forgive those who are actually killing Him, we should be able to forgive those who sin against us. Christ's example provides dimensions and understanding to the command not present in the abstract command itself.

The same holds true for the examples in the churches. It is one thing to read God's commands for how churches should function; it is far more illustrative to see these commands in action (or, negatively, to see how the churches fail to observe the commands). It is one thing, for instance, to see how God commands churches to support the promotion of the Gospel (1 Cor 9.1–14); it is another thing to see how a church like Antioch devotes itself to the Gospel and the fruit of that devotion (*cf.* Acts 13.1–3, *etc.*).

We must remember that God provided these examples for our understanding. Paul makes it clear to his audience that what was "written aforetime [was] for our learning" (Rom 15.3) and that things that happened in the past to Israel (*i.e.*, their example) "were written for our admonition" (1 Cor 10.11). If Paul used the examples of the past in this way to exhort the Christians of his own day, how much more then should we use the examples of the churches in the first century to exhort one another today? If it were true that the Old Testament and its examples were written for our learning and admonition, how much more then was the New Testament along with its examples written for the same purposes?

Examples, figurative language, and other often maligned aspects of the Scriptures are not accidental or unnecessary. They represent part of God's revealed will to us that we may learn, understand, and apply to our own lives, both as individuals and as local churches. We can see, then, that it is good for us to consider the examples of the churches of the New Testament, and that there is good reason to strive to conform to the New Testament churches as much as possible.

The New Testament Churches

How can we understand the examples of the New Testament churches? We have at our disposal the New Testament, geographic information, and demographic information from history. Within the New Testament, we have the Gospels which provide the instructions of Jesus that would have been given in the churches, the book of Acts that describes the origins and events within some of the churches, and the letters of the apostles, many of which were written to local churches.

Providing a coherent and understandable picture of the churches will require us to engage in historical reconstruction. We will use the available sources to establish a historically plausible and likely picture of each individual New Testament church which we will study. This type of investigation is often required, especially when we do not have all of the information that we would like. The need for historical reconstruction should not provide too much cause for concern; it is almost always necessary to provide a meaningful picture of any historical person, group, or event. Just as a parent can walk into a room and see markings on the wall, a marker on the ground, and markings on a child's hand, and from this deduce that the child took the marker and wrote on the wall, we can take all the information in the New Testament and put the story together as best we can.

This endeavor requires some disclaimers before we begin. First, the picture that is presented only represents the revealed information. We must freely admit that there might be aspects of the churches left unrevealed; there is not much we can do about that. We will do what we can to present the most coherent picture possible with all available information. Likewise, just as any individual local church today has a wide variety of individuals—all of whom possess different levels of maturity and different strengths and weaknesses—we must assume the same is true in the churches of the New Testament. Perhaps not every member of each local church deserves the commendations provided; likewise, not every member may deserve the rebuke or criticism given to the whole. Even though we must bear in mind some of the limitations of the study, we can have confidence that what can be known will be very profitable to understand.

The New Testament Church?

As we strive to understand the churches of the New Testament based upon the revelations in the Scriptures, we also must grapple with a more fundamental question in our quest: is it really possible for any church to truly be *the* New Testament church?

The question must be raised, for as we shall see, there are no two local churches that were alike. Each was different in its composition, location, strengths, and weaknesses.

We must consider, therefore, whether we should strive to create a picture of one coherent church and call it "the New Testament church" (*i.e.*, to add up all the strengths and commendations of the churches, along with the negatives to avoid, and consider it the "ideal" church), or whether we should look at each individual church as "paradigmatic New Testament churches" (*i.e.*, to consider each church, consider its strengths and weaknesses, and use each as a paradigm through which we can compare churches today), or perhaps a blend of the two approaches. This is not a question that we will consider in depth at this point, but must be kept in mind as we proceed.

Let us now begin our investigation with the historical analysis of the churches as revealed in the New Testament.

Jerusalem

"But ye shall receive power, when the Holy Spirit is come upon you: and ye shall be my witnesses both in Jerusalem, and in all Judaea and Samaria, and unto the uttermost part of the earth." (Acts 1.8)

Jerusalem (translated, "foundation of peace") occupies a unique role in the Scriptures as the center of Jewish life and religion. It is the City of David, the city of the prophets, and the final destination for Jesus in His ministry. It is fitting that God determined to begin Christ's church in Jerusalem, the city of the Temple and beacon for all Jews. Unfortunately, however, the city's fate was sealed even before the church began.

Geography and History

By all accounts, one would not expect Jerusalem to be a major capital city. It is not located on any major road system, nor is it on a major body of water. Jerusalem is in the hill country of Judah in modern Israel, approximately 2,500 feet above sea level, right on the crest of the mountains (hence people "going down" from Jerusalem or "going up" to Jerusalem; *cf.* Acts 8.15; 21.15; *etc.*). The city is 33 miles east of the Mediterranean Sea and 15 miles west of the northern end of the Dead Sea. In Old Testament times, Jerusalem was on the border of the territory of Judah and Benjamin, although technically it was in Benjamin proper (*cf.* Josh 18.11–20). The Gihon Spring provided a constant source of water, and the city was afforded some protection with deep valleys to its south, west, and east.

Jerusalem is an old city. Abraham was met there by the king of Salem, Melchizedek, who was also priest of God Most High (*ca.* 2000 BCE; Gen 14.18–20). Later on the city was inhabited by Jebusites, even after the Israelite conquest (Jdg 1.21). David famously captured the city around 1000 BCE (*cf.* 2 Sam 5.6–10); he established Jerusalem as his capital since it was on the border of Benjamin and Judah and had not been possessed by any individual tribe of the Israelites before that time. David's son Solomon built a Temple to YHWH in Jerusalem not many years later (*cf.* 1 Kings 6), and from then on Jerusalem was firmly established as the political and religious center of Judah.

After Solomon's rule Israel was divided into two nations: the ten tribes of the north and Judah in the south (1 Kings 11–12); Jerusalem remained the capital of the Kingdom of Judah until 586 BCE, when the Babylonians razed the city and the Temple to the ground (2 Chron 36.17–21). After the end of the exile, many Jews returned and re-built both the city and the Temple (Ezra 1–2; 6.13–18). Except for a short period of self-rule from 167 to 63 BCE, the land of Judah was part of the successive empires of the Persians, Ptolemies, Seleucids, and Romans.

Jerusalem factored heavily in the life and ministry of Jesus of Nazareth. He was presented in the Temple as a youth, taught in the Temple at age twelve (*cf.* Luke 2), and traveled there during the major festivals. Jesus knew full well that He would go and die in Jerusalem (Luke 13.31–35). After He symbolically purged the Temple and predicted the impending doom of Jerusalem around the year 30 CE, the rulers of the Jews conspired to have Him tried and executed (Luke 20–23). On the third day after His crucifixion, Jesus of Nazareth was raised from the dead in Jerusalem and established that His disciples would begin His work from there (Luke 24; Acts 1.1–8).

As the center of Jewish life, Jerusalem was always a hotbed for insurrection and Jewish national aspirations. The city was overwhelmingly Jewish, and many Jews resented the perceived oppression they received at the hands of the Roman authorities. The city often saw revolts and uprisings, and the citizens felt the Roman military presence often. It was within this climate that the apostles began proclaiming the Kingdom of God.

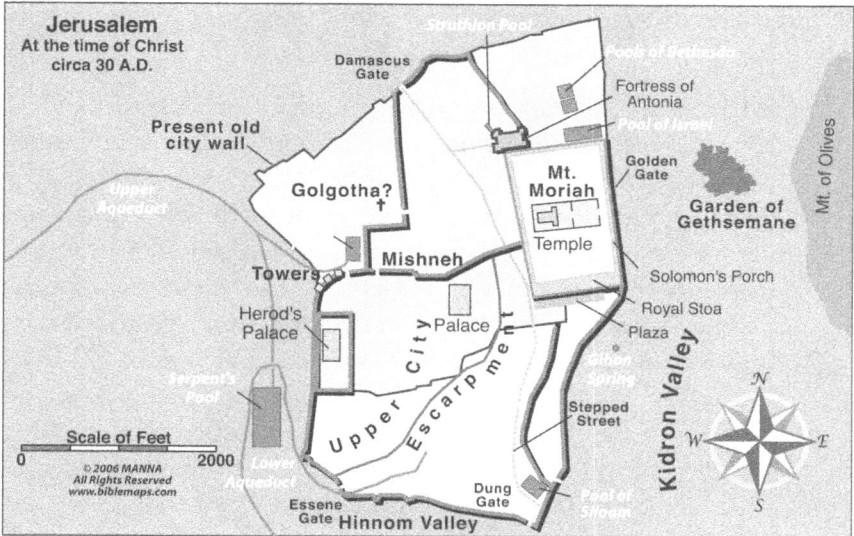

The Earliest Church (30–31/33)

The church in Jerusalem began in the year 30 on the day of Pentecost, as recorded in Acts 2. The Holy Spirit fell upon the twelve apostles, and they began to speak in tongues (Acts 2.1–7). Peter stood in their midst and presented the first Gospel lesson, and 3,000 were baptized as a result (Acts 2.14–41). While some of the converts were native inhabitants of Jerusalem, we see in Acts 2.8–11 that Jews from many other nations who had come to Jerusalem for the festival were present, and heard the message; undoubtedly, many of them were part of the 3,000. We are given a wonderful description of this church in Acts 2.42–47:

> And they continued stedfastly in the apostles' teaching and fellowship, in the breaking of bread and the prayers. And fear came upon every soul: and many wonders and signs were done by the apostles. And all that believed were together, and had all things common; and they sold their possessions and goods, and parted them to all, according as any man had need. And day by day, continuing stedfastly with one accord in the temple, and breaking bread at home, they did take their food with gladness and singleness of heart, praising God, and having favour with

all the people. And the Lord added to them day by day those that were being saved.

Many details are provided: they spent their time together and devoted themselves to learning the truth of God from the apostles, to prayer, to the Lord's Supper, and to association with the apostles and with one another. While we do not know exactly how long some of the converts from other nations stayed in Jerusalem, it seems clear that they stayed longer than they had originally intended and that this situation called for Christians to sell their possessions so that none would be in need (*cf.* Acts 4.32–37). They assembled in various parts of the Temple and in homes, and on account of the signs and wonders of the apostles, the preaching of Christ, and the example of the believers, many were added to their number: 3,000 soon became well over 5,000 (Acts 4.4).

The earliest church thus met an extraordinary situation with extraordinary solutions, both in terms of being marvelous and being outside the norm. The picture of harmony that is presented does not last forever; we learn that some disputes arise between native Israelite Jews and the more Greek (or Hellenistic) Jews regarding the distribution of food to widows in Acts 6.1. After some servants were selected to handle the matter, the church was strengthened and even some of the priests became obedient to Christ (Acts 6.2–7).

The presentation of the church in Jerusalem in the earliest years is compelling: these Jews who heard and believed that Jesus of Nazareth was indeed their Messiah quickly showed extraordinary love and levels of association with their fellow believers; therefore, it should come as no surprise that such a group was attractive to many and that the number of Christians quickly grew.

The Middle Years (31/33–61)
Unfortunately, this idyllic church situation could not last. Somewhere between 31 and 33, Stephen, one of the seven servants, was brought before the Jewish council (or Sanhedrin) on trumped-up charges (Acts 6.8–15). Stephen defiantly preached the Gospel and condemned the rulers, and he was stoned as a result (Acts 7).

On that day a great persecution of the church arose in Jerusalem, and we are told that only the apostles remained in Jerusalem (Acts 8.1). While this persecution was made into a benefit for the church universal, since Christians were scattered throughout Samaria and Judea and the whole world promoting the Gospel, it seems to have caused great difficulty in Jerusalem proper. (If any of the people from the various nations who had come to Jerusalem for Pentecost were left after one to three years, they had almost certainly returned to their homeland.) It is likely that many Christians returned to Jerusalem after Saul's persecutions ended (*cf.* Acts 9.31) and that many others were converted in Jerusalem, so that James can speak of "thousands" of brethren among the Jews twenty years later (Acts 21.20). Nevertheless, we can perceive from the historical accounts that the church was going through some difficulties in this period.

It is apparent that persecution often plagued the church. We see it explicitly with the arrest of Peter and James (the brother of John), leading to James' execution, sometime between 42–44 (Acts 12.1–3) and also with the death of James the Just, the brother of the Lord, around 61 (Josephus, *Antiquities of the Jews*, 20.9; Eusebius, *Ecclesiastical History*, 2.9). We should not think, however, that only the Jerusalem Christians were persecuted at these times. The book of Acts constantly records the adversity suffered by Paul and others at the hands of the Jews when preaching the Gospel (*e.g.*, Acts 17); if this was true of the Jews of the Diaspora, how much more would it be true in the heartland of the Jews? The church in Jerusalem most likely constantly suffered harassment from the Jews around them.

The church in Jerusalem posed difficulties for the Kingdom overall in terms of a doctrinal disputation that arose. While the church was thoroughly Jewish, all was well, although we should note that there were even difficulties between native Jews and diaspora Jews (*cf.* Acts 6.1). According to Acts 10, however, God demonstrated to Peter that the Gentiles should be allowed to hear the Gospel and become Christians. The Christians in Jerusalem called him to task immediately on his return (Acts 11.1) and at the time seemed to assent to the promotion of the Gospel to the Gentiles (Acts 11.18).

It soon became apparent, however, that acceptance of the Gentiles represents a major issue that must be resolved: should the Gentiles be compelled to observe the Law of Moses? Some Jewish Christians, notably of the sect of the Pharisees (*cf.* Acts 15.5), believed that all believing Gentiles should be subjected to the Law of Moses; consequently, some of them went to Antioch around the year 50 and taught as much (Acts 15.1). Paul and Barnabas challenged this view, and it was determined that the matter should be resolved in Jerusalem (Acts 15.2). It is established in Acts 11.29–30 that there were elders shepherding the flock in Jerusalem by 41–44, and James the brother of the Lord was prominent among them (Acts 15.13; Gal 2.9). The apostles and elders come together to discuss these matters, and the determination made with the guidance of the Holy Spirit was that the Law of Moses was not to be bound upon the Gentile believers (Acts 15.6–29). Nevertheless, some of the Jewish Christians proved disobedient to this determination, and from Paul's letters to the churches of Galatia, Corinth, Rome, and Colossae, we can discern that Judaizing controversies occurred in these churches. Paul did not have nice words for such people: he called them "false brethren" (Gal 2.4) and constantly opposed their teachings. Even if not every Judaizing teacher came from Jerusalem, the presence of Jerusalem, the Temple complex, and the example of the Christians of Jerusalem provided the fuel to fan that doctrinal controversy. Jerusalem was thus the center of the great doctrinal disputation of the early years of the church.

The clearest picture of the church in Jerusalem at this time is presented in Acts 21.19–24, around 57–59. Paul had returned to Jerusalem after his missionary journeys to present the benevolence from the churches of Greece (Acts 20–21; Rom 15.25) and was greatly concerned about how he would be welcomed, going so far as to ask the Roman brethren to pray for him in this regard (*cf.* Rom 15.31–32). Luke records the event for us in Acts 21.19–24:

And when he had saluted them, he rehearsed one by one the things which God had wrought among the Gentiles by his ministry.

And they, when they heard it, glorified God; and they said unto him, "Thou seest, brother, how many thousands there are among the Jews of them which have believed; and they are all zealous for the law: and they have been informed concerning thee, that thou teachest all the Jews which are among the Gentiles to forsake Moses, telling them not to circumcise their children, neither to walk after the customs. What is it therefore? they will certainly hear that thou art come. Do therefore this that we say to thee: We have four men which have a vow on them; these take, and purify thyself with them, and be at charges for them, that they may shave their heads: and all shall know that there is no truth in the things whereof they have been informed concerning thee; but that thou thyself also walkest orderly, keeping the law."

Now we can better understand Paul's concerns: he did not have the best report in Jerusalem! We learn here that the Jewish Christians are "all zealous for the law" and that they have heard that Paul has induced the Jewish Christians in the diaspora to forsake the Law of Moses. While we do not see Paul explicitly teaching this anywhere, one could certainly come to this conclusion from such statements as Romans 7.1–6 and Galatians 3–4. The Jewish Christians asked Paul to purify himself in the Temple and to act like a good Jew to quell the rumors; according to Acts 21.26–28, he did so.

What should we make of this? There has been no end of controversy as to whether Paul sinned by doing what he did. Since Luke recorded these events without providing any hint of disapproval of either the Jewish Christians in Jerusalem or of Paul, it is difficult to charge either with sin; nevertheless, it is clear that the situation of the church in Jerusalem is far different from the situation of any other church. Whether right or wrong, the Christians in Jerusalem strove both to follow Jesus as the Christ and to maintain the customs of the Jewish Law. Their zeal seems to be directed toward the customs of their forefathers, and we can detect a note of opposition to Paul's teachings that Christ has abrogated the Law for His followers. This sentiment was so strong that Paul was compelled to go along with them and not to stand against them; this was entirely in line with his being "as a Jew" to win over Jews (1 Cor 9.20). As we will see, however, the focus of the church in Jerusalem seems to be too much on its Jewishness and on the "customs of the forefathers" and not on Christ and the Gospel.

The End of Jerusalem (61–70)

In 61, the death of James resulted in a time of transition for the church in Jerusalem. If Peter had not yet left Jerusalem by this time, he would within the next few years. We do not know when the other apostles left Jerusalem, but it would seem that most left by 65–67.

Tensions in Jerusalem were mounting. The Romans did many things to offend the Jews, and the depravity of the Roman governors of the province became too much for them to bear. In 66 the Jews in Jerusalem revolted from Roman rule; by the year 70, the destruction that Jesus predicted in Matthew 24.1–36, Mark 13, and Luke 21 had come to pass. At some point between 66 and 70, the Jewish Christians evacuated Jerusalem and traveled to Pella in the Transjordan Decapolis, heeding the warning of the Lord (Luke 21.34–36; Eusebius, *Ecclesiastical History* 3.5.3; Epiphanius, *Of Weights and Measures* 15). With the city destroyed and the Temple gone, never to be rebuilt, the church in Jerusalem as it existed beforehand was no more. We are told that some of the Christians eventually did return to Jerusalem, and since the city was opened up to the Gentiles, the church in Jerusalem most likely became much like the other, mostly Gentile, churches. The Jewish Christian stronghold was gone, and the covenant with Israel was fully superseded (Heb 7–9).

We learn of the church in Jerusalem of this period from the letter to the Hebrews. The greatest consensus is that the author was writing to the Christians in Judea, of which Jerusalem was no doubt the center. The letter seems to have been written after the death of James but before the destruction of Jerusalem and is best dated between 64 and 67.

From the Hebrew letter we gain a distressing picture: many of the Christians there were immature, discouraged in the faith, and needed strengthening. The Hebrew author chastised the brethren in Hebrews 5.12–6.4 for still needing the "milk" of the Word when they ought to have been teachers. Considering that it was possible that some of those who converted on the day of Pentecost or soon after were still alive and that no church was older than the church in Jerusalem, this criticism seems just. It indicates that more time was perhaps spent on Jewish custom than on the "elementary doctrines" of Christ.

It should not surprise us that in the midst of the great tumult in Jerusalem, with the church having lost many of its "pillars," that discouragement should set in. The Hebrew author urged the brethren to encourage one another lest any be hardened and fall away (Heb 3.12–14). He encouraged them to remember how much greater are the promises of the covenant with Christ than the covenant with Israel (Heb 2.2–4; 3.1–6). He admonished them to remain faithful to receive the rest their fathers never entered (Heb 4.1–11). He reminded them that they had not yet resisted to the point of blood, and that they should not faint under the discipline of God, but rather be strengthened (Heb 12.3–29). He pleaded with them to remember how they had survived previous persecution, had helped others before them survive persecution, and to persevere again (Heb 10.32–33). The day of the end of Jerusalem was near, and the brethren had to encourage one another (Heb 10.24–25). The entire letter was designed to demonstrate the superiority of the covenant between God and man through Christ Jesus over the covenant between God and Israel and to show how the latter was passing away.

We can only hope that the letter was received favorably and that the Christians in Jerusalem remained steadfast until they left for Pella. The situation of the church in Jerusalem, nevertheless, demonstrates that persecution and difficulty can lead to despair, especially when Christians are not as well-versed in God's Word as they ought to be.

Conclusion

The church in Jerusalem as described in the New Testament lasted for only forty years and went through three distinct phases in its life. We see in its example some of the greatest moments and examples of the faith: the earliest church with its love and association, a church that survives despite constant persecution and harassment. We also see a church conforming to its environment; zealous for the Law of Moses and for Jewish customs, the church became the center of great doctrinal dispute that was a stumbling-block for the Kingdom as a whole while misdirecting its own spiritual strength. The church that began with such great power and energy in Acts 2 was weak and discouraged by the time the author of Hebrews wrote his epistle. The church in Jerusalem demonstrates the importance of love, association, prayer, and devotion to the apostles' doctrine for proper and continual growth in a church. It further reinforces how Christ must always be the head and focus of the church if it will be successful (*cf.* Acts 2.42; Eph 5.22–33).

Antioch

…and that the disciples were called Christians first in Antioch. (Acts 11.26c)

It is entirely appropriate that those who followed Christ were first called Christians in Antioch, the first city in which Jews and Gentiles truly came together to become one group. The implications of the Gentiles' access to the Gospel after the events of Acts 10 were momentous, and they were quickly and greatly realized in Antioch.

Geography and History

Antioch of Syria (modern Antakya in Turkey) is situated in the uppermost part of the Levant, about 15 miles inland from the Mediterranean Sea on the Orontes River and approximately 300 miles north of Jerusalem. Only a small village throughout the Old Testament period, the city was ideally suited as a major center: the Orontes River was navigable to the Mediterranean, and it cut a valley through the mountain valleys that allowed easy passage for caravans from the Euphrates region and points further east. Likewise, major roads from the areas of western Turkey, Egypt and Palestine converged at Antioch. Antioch thus became a major trading and commerce center.

The city owes its prominence to the founder of the Macedonian Seleucid dynasty, Seleucus I, who made it the capital of his empire around 300 BCE. Settled by Greek soldiers, Jewish colonists, and native Syrians, Antioch quickly grew and developed into one of a select few major trading centers of the eastern Mediterranean.

Antioch and Alexandria in Egypt became the greatest cities of the eastern Mediterranean world.

During Roman times the city had a very mixed population that included both Jews and Gentiles. The city is often portrayed as containing great debauchery, yet it does not seem any more depraved than any other major metropolitan area of the first century. Nevertheless, Antioch represented extremely fertile ground for the promotion of the Gospel.

The Church in Antioch

Although not much is presented in the Scriptures regarding the church in Antioch, what is revealed indicates the great importance of Antioch in our study of the churches of the New Testament. We first read about Antioch in Acts 11.19:

> They therefore that were scattered abroad upon the tribulation that arose about Stephen travelled as far as Phoenicia, and Cyprus, and Antioch, speaking the word to none save only to Jews.

We remember that after Stephen's stoning in 31–33 CE in Acts 7, a great persecution arose against the church in Jerusalem and the brethren were scattered about the countryside. We know that Philip went to Samaria, Azotus and Caesarea (Acts 8), and that in Acts 11, Luke returns to the story of the rest of those scattered here. We do not know exactly when those who were scattered about reached Antioch: it could be argued that it would have taken time for some brethren to travel 300 miles while preaching the Gospel, but we also know that some of those who were present in the church in Jerusalem hailed from Antioch (Nicolaus the proselyte, Acts 6.5) and that such persons may have immediately traveled on to their home city. We will consider the events of Acts 11.19 occurring, then, around 32–35.

In the beginning the Gospel was only promoted to the Jews of Antioch. After the conversion of Cornelius, however, we hear that some of the converted Jews who originally hailed from Cyprus and Cyrene began preaching the Gospel to the Greeks as well, and many were converted (Acts 11.20–21). When the report

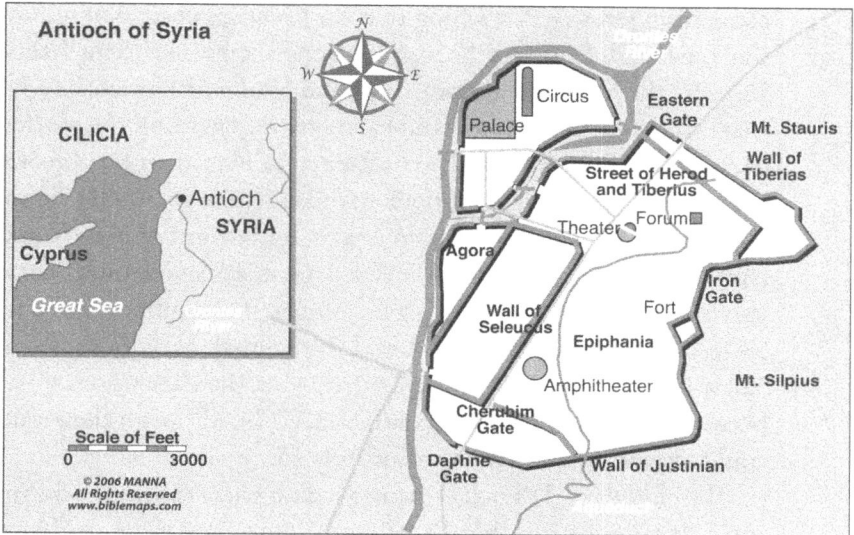

reached Jerusalem, the church there sent Barnabas to Antioch (Acts 11.22). Barnabas was manifestly impressed with what he saw; while he would travel to Jerusalem for certain errands, Antioch became his "home church," so to speak. He went to get Saul from Tarsus, and they both remained in Antioch for some time (Acts 11.23–26). When a prophet from Jerusalem predicted famine for the whole land, the church in Antioch prepared a contribution for the brethren in Judea, which was duly given during the famine, *ca.* 41–44 (Acts 11.27–30). These events are very difficult to date: Cornelius was most likely converted sometime between 37 and 41, and these events occurred right after his conversion. We can see, then, that the church in Antioch was exclusively Jewish for a period of time between two and nine years before the Gentiles were brought into the faith.

Antioch is again mentioned in Acts 13.1–4 as having prophets and teachers, and from them the Holy Spirit separated Paul and Barnabas to preach the Gospel in other lands between 44 and 46. From Antioch began what is popularly called the first missionary journey. After Paul and Barnabas' return, Antioch became the center of the Judaizing controversy: some Jewish Christians came from Jerusalem teaching that the Gentiles needed to follow the Law, and Paul and Barnabas strongly opposed them (Acts 15.1–2). The church determined to send Paul and Barnabas to Jerusalem to ask the apostles and elders there regarding the matter (Acts 15.2). The result of the conference in Jerusalem (*ca.* 48–50) compelled the church in Antioch to rejoice (Acts 15.30–31). Soon after this, Paul and Barnabas split ways on account of John Mark (Acts 15.36–40), and Paul departed on his second missionary journey around 50–51. Paul again returned to Antioch in Acts 18.18–23, between the second and third missionary journeys in 52; it is most likely around this time that the dissension arose between Peter and Paul in Galatians 2.11–14, although the event could also be dated to the time of Acts 15.

The church in Antioch is mentioned nowhere else in the Scriptures. It would seem that Peter spent some time there, perhaps even serving as an elder (*cf.* Gal 2.11). Sadly, it would be a later "bishop" of Antioch, Ignatius, who would strongly promote the elevation of one bishop over a collective of elders around 115.

The Church in Antioch: A Model of Cooperation

We have seen that Antioch was a melting pot of different cultures and religions, and that people from different geographical and religious backgrounds comprised the church there. Men and women from all over the eastern Mediterranean world made up the church in Antioch, including a variety of people from all kinds of social backgrounds—regular people for sure, but also the foster-brother of Herod the tetrarch (Acts 13.1).

Perhaps the greatest challenge faced by the church in Antioch was the consolidation of both Jews and Gentiles into one body. As we will see, many other churches faced quarrels and controversies on account of the historical distinctions between Jews and Gentiles, and yet we see little of that in Antioch. The exceptions, in fact, prove the rule: the only controversies that arose between Jews and Gentiles in Antioch resulted from influences from Jerusalem (Acts 15.1; Gal 2.11–14). This is all the more surprising when we recognize that Antioch was one of the first churches to struggle with the integration of Jews and Gentiles, especially since there were Jewish Christians there for years before the Gentiles were added to the fold! Nevertheless, it is clear that the brethren in Antioch were willing to submit to God and His will above their own ethnic divisions and that such a willingness led to wonderful things.

The church in Antioch thus represents a model of cooperation among brethren. Antioch demonstrated that it was possible for Jews and Gentiles to put aside the animosities that had characterized the previous few hundred years and work together in serving the Lord.

Their example, no doubt, provided encouragement to Paul and Barnabas. As was noted, Barnabas was sent from Jerusalem to Antioch, and the situation he found impressed him enough to lead him not only to stay there but also to bring in Paul. It is little wonder that Paul and Barnabas then went out and preached the Gospel to parts of Asia Minor and Greece, attempting to bring together Jews and Gentiles to form churches in those lands. They knew that Jews and Gentiles could be Christians together, and Antioch had been their training ground.

The Church in Antioch: Focused on the Gospel

Perhaps part of the success of the integration of Jews and Gentiles in Antioch was due to their focus on the Gospel. Teaching was a constant theme involved with the church in Antioch; all the significant passages speaking of the church in Antioch mention it (Acts 11; 13; 15). Exhortation was also highly significant to the church in Antioch, and the message of the Gospel seems to have been heard. When the Spirit called Paul and Barnabas to preach in other places, the brethren in Antioch did not seem to complain about losing great teachers, but willingly sent them off to further the Gospel message. Paul also constantly returned to Antioch to visit the brethren and to report concerning the work he was doing (*cf.* Acts 14.26–28; Acts 18.18). The Gospel—living its message and promoting it—was highly regarded in Antioch, and such led to the success of the church in no small measure.

The church in Antioch thus represents a dynamic group of believers focused on the promotion of the Gospel and association amongst one another. Despite all kinds of differences and potential difficulties that sidelined other churches, Antioch stood firm and became a beacon of integration and evangelism. Antioch can demonstrate to us that as long as a church is focused on the Gospel message, all kinds of differences and difficulties can be overcome.

Galatia

O foolish Galatians, who did bewitch you, before whose eyes Jesus Christ was openly set forth crucified? (Gal 3.1)

Many of the churches of Galatia represent some of the firstfruits of the missionary work of Paul and Barnabas. The New Testament records that Paul often visited these churches, yet never had the opportunity to spend much time with them. Unfortunately, to Paul's complete surprise, certain "Judaizing" teachers infiltrated the Galatian region and compelled Paul to write a letter exhorting the Christians of Galatia to return to the primitive and true Gospel.

Geography and History

Galatia can refer to either an ethnic area or a province of the Roman Empire. Both may be found within the center of the Anatolian peninsula (modern-day Turkey); the ethnic area is the northern section ("north Galatia"), while the province also included the areas of Lycaonia and Pisidia ("south Galatia"). While there is some contention over how Paul uses the term "Galatia," it seems from the whole of the New Testament that he speaks in terms of Roman provinces (*cf.* Macedonia, Achaia [2 Cor 1.1, 16], Asia [2 Cor 1.8]), and therefore it is best to establish that Paul is writing to the entire Roman province.

In the days of the Exodus of the Israelites, Galatia was the center of the Hittite Empire, and it was populated by native Anatolians until the third century BCE, when a wave of Celtic invaders from Gaul (modern-day France) conquered and settled down within the center of the Anatolian peninsula. "Galatia" receives its name from these Gauls. The land was full of Gentiles and their pagan religions, although there were some Jews in the land, especially in the southern section of the province.

Chronology of the Letter to the Galatians

Before we begin our analysis of the churches of Galatia as represented in the New Testament, it is advisable to recognize the complications and difficulties inherent in attempting to reconcile the chronology of the Galatian letter with the chronology of the book of Acts. There are many different ways in which the two may be reconciled; none of this changes the truth within either book, but the way in which the churches are perceived and historically reconstructed will differ based upon which option is believed.

In Galatians 1–2, Paul sets out part of the history of his conversion and interaction with brethren in Jerusalem. According to some, all of these events occur within the timeframe of Acts 9–11, from Paul's conversion to Paul's mission to Jerusalem to deliver the aid from the brethren in Antioch, and therefore Paul writes Galatians from Antioch just before the council of Acts 15. While this view would resolve some of the interpretive questions within the book, I find the argument unconvincing historically. The most natural reading of Galatians 1–2 has Paul in Jerusalem three years from his conversion and then again fourteen years after that point; such brings us to about 48–50, the time of the Acts 15 council. This means that Paul writes Galatians after this event, either sometime between 49–51 or 55–57, and I believe that the latter is the most likely. There are many correlations between 1 and 2 Corinthians and Galatians: Cephas is mentioned in both (Gal 2.1, 1 Cor 1.12), instruction given to the "churches of Galatia" is also given to Corinth (1 Cor 16.1), 2 Corinthians and Galatians handle matters regarding "Judaizing" teachers, and Paul uses the same image of leaven and dough in Galatians 5.9 and 1 Corinthians 5.6. As we continue in our analysis, we will assume a date of writing around 55–57 from Ephesus, which will function as the foundation of our historical reconstruction.

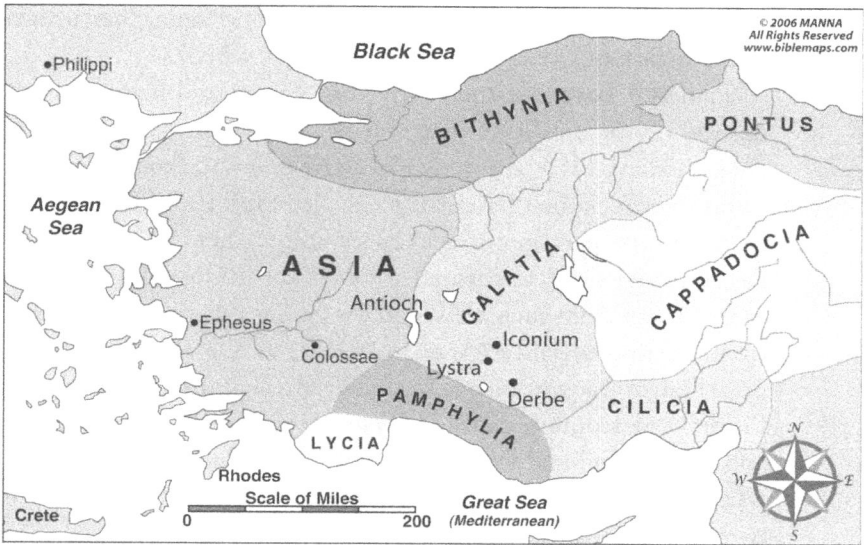

The Churches of Galatia in the First Missionary Journey

As we previously saw in our study of Antioch of Syria, Paul and Barnabas were set aside by the Holy Spirit for missionary endeavor in Antioch in around 46 (Acts 13.1–3). From Antioch they traveled to Cyprus, and then to the Anatolian peninsula through Pamphylia (Acts 13.4–14). Barnabas and Paul then travel to Antioch of Pisidia, within the province of Galatia, and here they begin preaching the Gospel in Galatia (Acts 13.14). They begin, as is Paul's custom, in the synagogue of the Jews, where Paul preaches a masterful lesson from the Old Testament demonstrating how Jesus of Nazareth is the Christ (Acts 13.15–41). The Jews were willing to hear more of Paul until the Gentiles arrived to hear the Gospel; the Jews then turned on Paul and stirred up persecution against them (Acts 13.42–52). Nevertheless, perhaps some of the Jews—and certainly many of the Gentiles—were converted, and a church was established there (Acts 13.48, 52).

From Antioch of Pisidia Paul and Barnabas traveled to Iconium, and again preached in the synagogues, but this time met with more success (Acts 14.1). They stayed longer in Iconium than in Antioch of Pisidia, but again the Jews rise up against Paul and

Barnabas, and when a plan is hatched to stone them, they depart to the region of Lycaonia in Galatia (Acts 14.2–6).

Paul and Barnabas then arrived in Lystra and began preaching the Gospel. When a man was healed of infirmity there, the people believed that the gods had come down to them in human form. They reckoned Barnabas to be Zeus and Paul Hermes, and even made preparations to make sacrifices to them (Acts 14.6–13). Paul quickly strives to persuade them that the Gospel is preached to free them from such views, and is barely able to restrain them from offering sacrifice (Acts 14.14–18). While the Gospel was preached in Lystra and some believed, Jews from Antioch of Pisidia and Iconium came to Lystra, persuaded the multitudes, and stoned Paul and left him for dead (Acts 14.19–20). Paul and Barnabas then go to Derbe of Lycaonia in Galatia and preach there (Acts 14.21).

From Derbe Paul and Barnabas return to Lystra, Iconium, and Antioch of Pisidia, strengthening the disciples, exhorting them to recognize that through tribulation we enter the Kingdom of God, and then appointing elders for each church (Acts 14.21–23). Afterward Paul and Barnabas return to Antioch of Syria through Pamphylia.

The churches of Antioch of Pisidia, Iconium, Lystra, and Derbe, then, are the sum—or at least the starting nucleus—of the churches of Galatia. While Paul and Barnabas diligently labored to preach the Word of God in these communities, they suffered persecution at almost every turn, and doubtless the disciples in these communities continued to suffer at the hands of the Jews. Nevertheless, many did believe the Gospel, and the churches were left with proper Biblical leadership.

Paul and the Churches of Galatia, 48–55

After the contention in Antioch and Jerusalem over the Gentiles and the Law of Moses, Paul returned to the churches of Galatia around 49–50, delivering the decree of the Holy Spirit and strengthening the disciples (Acts 16.1–6). We also learn that Timothy, one of Paul's most trusted associates, comes from Lystra in Galatia, and he began to travel with Paul after Paul circumcised him on account of the Jews in that place (Acts 16.1–3).

After his travels through Macedonia, Achaia, Asia, and Syria, Paul again returns to the churches of Galatia as he is traveling to Ephesus around 53–54 (Acts 18.23). He again works to strengthen the disciples, and perhaps it is at this time that he provides the instructions for the collection (1 Cor 16.1).

The New Testament does not record any other visits by Paul to the churches in Galatia. While it is possible that Paul might have visited them between his Roman imprisonments (*ca.* 62–64), it is most likely that the Galatians never saw Paul in the flesh again.

In 2 Timothy 4.10, Paul records that Crescens, one of his associates, was off in Galatia around 64; likewise, Galatia is one of the regions to which Peter addresses his letter in 1 Peter 1.1. Such, save the letter to which we now turn, is what we know of the churches of Galatia from the New Testament.

Galatia and the Judaizing Apostasy

At some point soon after Paul's last visit to the Galatian region, some "Judaizing" teachers, perhaps from Jerusalem but most certainly Jewish Christians, came to Galatia and began to preach that the Gentile Christians should be circumcised and to observe at least parts of the traditions of the Jews (Gal 1.6–9; 4.8–10). The matter became contentious (Gal 5.16), and yet the "Judaizing" teachers gained the upper hand. The authenticity of the Gospel that Paul preached to the Galatians was now in doubt: the "Judaizers" claimed that his gospel came from men, not God, and too influenced by brethren in Antioch and not Jerusalem (*cf.* Gal 1.11–12).

Paul, in Ephesus, hears of this at some point between 55 and 57, and is stunned. He is amazed that despite so many years of faithfulness in the Gospel that they would so quickly turn to another gospel (Gal 1.6), and is perplexed at how they would believe these "Judaizers" (Gal 4.20). Unable to be present to handle the matter in person (*cf.* Gal 4.20), Paul sends out a sharp letter to defend himself and the true Gospel. His Gospel is not from men but of God, and he lays out how he received the Gospel by revelation and later conferred with brethren in Jerusalem (Gal 1.1–2.10). He even establishes how he opposed Cephas in Antioch for his hypocrisy in the face of Christians from Jerusalem (Gal 2.11–14; Eusebius of Caesarea's claim from Clement of Alexandria [*Eccl. Hist.* 1.12.3] that "Cephas" here is another disciple and not Peter is hard to reconcile with Paul's interchanging use of "Peter" and "Cephas" in Galatians 1.18, 2.7, and 2.9, let alone the idea that a "Cephas" who is not Peter would be a "pillar" with James and John in Galatians 2.9). Paul then deftly demonstrates the superiority of the covenant with Christ and how the old covenant has passed away (Gal 3). Furthermore, to submit to circumcision is to be subject to the whole law and a falling from grace (Gal 5.1–4). We can feel Paul's pain and frustration with the Galatians from Galatians 4.8–20 and Galatians 5.7–11:

> Howbeit at that time, not knowing God, ye were in bondage to them that by nature are no gods: but now that ye have come to know God, or rather to be known by God, how turn ye back again to the weak and beggarly rudiments, whereunto ye desire to be in bondage over again? Ye observe days, and months, and seasons, and years. I am afraid of you, lest by any means I have bestowed labor upon you in vain. I beseech you, brethren, become as I am, for I also am become as ye are. Ye did me no wrong: but ye know that because of an infirmity of the flesh I preached the gospel unto you the first time: and that which was a temptation to you in my flesh ye despised not, nor rejected; but ye received me as an angel of God, even as Christ Jesus. Where then is that gratulation of yourselves? For I bear you witness, that, if possible, ye would have plucked out your eyes and given them to me. So then am I become your enemy, by telling you the truth? They zealously seek you in no good way; nay, they desire to shut you out, that ye may seek them. But it is good to be zealously sought in a good matter at all times, and not only when I am present with you. My little children, of whom I am again in travail until Christ be formed in you—but I could wish to be present with you now, and to change my tone; for I am perplexed about you.

Ye were running well; who hindered you that ye should not obey the truth? This persuasion came not of him that calleth you. A little leaven leaveneth the whole lump. I have confidence to you-ward in the Lord, that ye will be none otherwise minded: but he that troubleth you shall bear his judgment, whosoever he be. But I, brethren, if I still preach circumcision, why am I still persecuted? Then hath the stumbling-block of the cross been done away.

Paul is clearly pained that disciples for whom he diligently labored in the Lord and who previously approved of him have now seemed to turn against him and the true Gospel. The strength of Paul's rebuke in Galatians indicates a very strong relationship between himself and the Galatians; in other circumstances, like in 2 Corinthians, Paul does not speak nearly as sharply. It is clear, then, that this dissension came out of the blue and it distressed Paul greatly that Christians who should have known better would fall prey to false doctrines.

The fact that Paul sent Crescens to Galatia (2 Tim 4.10) is good evidence that the Galatians received his letter as intended and repented of having listened to the "Judaizers." Nevertheless, the example of the churches of Galatia provides a good warning to always be on guard for false doctrines.

General Instruction in Galatians

The letter to the Galatians also records for us many of the teachings that Paul would present to the churches of the New Testament. We should not assume that their presence in the letter to the Galatians means that the Galatians had more difficulties with these matters than other churches; Paul simply takes the opportunity afforded him by the need to write the letter to remind the Galatians of important teachings (*cf.* Gal 5.21).

In Galatians 5.16–26, Paul encourages the brethren in Galatia to walk by the Spirit and not by the flesh. He clearly outlines the "works of the flesh" versus the "fruit of the Spirit," and demonstrates a commitment to proper Christian conduct. The thrust of Paul's message is seen in Galatians 5.24: "And they that are of Christ Jesus have crucified the flesh with the passions and the lusts thereof."

Paul placed great emphasis on proper personal conduct for all the brethren in the churches of Galatia and all the churches with whom he was associated.

In Galatians 6.1–10, Paul further encourages the brethren to restore any fallen brother, making sure that they themselves are also not tempted. He also establishes that Christians are to bear one another's burdens, and to always seek the good of those around them. One should not think highly of oneself but focus on what is good for everyone. Christians will reap what they have sowed, and therefore they ought to always be active in good works, helping those in need, especially in the household of God. Christians, then, are to be concerned for one another and for doing good and ought not focus on themselves.

Paul's concerns are manifest: Christians are to exhibit proper conduct in their personal morality, walking according to the Spirit, but no Christian should be so focused on himself so as to neglect the needs of others. Paul expects the brethren in Galatia to be concerned for one another and to be active in one another's lives, always abounding in good works of benevolence toward each other and those outside the fold in need. The brethren were indeed accountable to one another in Christ Jesus.

Conclusion

The churches in Galatia were established in the crucible of persecution, yet for many years were relatively stable in the faith. The evidence from Acts demonstrates the difficulties from Jews and Gentiles—Jews jealous of Gentiles and persecuting the work, Gentiles not understanding the nature of the Gospel—and yet for many years the churches of Galatia were successful and stood for the truth.

Nevertheless, when false teachers arrived, casting doubt on the truth and teaching error, the churches of Galatia accepted them. Paul had every reason to be dumbfounded and frustrated—the churches in Galatia had stood firm in the truth for about a decade, and within a very short time had accepted a false gospel. Paul never taught that the Gentiles required circumcision. The decree from Jerusalem was read to them, and they rejoiced in its comfort. Nevertheless, a few years later, they still accepted teachings contrary to these truths!

While we may be glad that the Galatians most likely repented of their errors, the churches of Galatia stand as a important reminder to us about the importance of constantly teaching the "whole counsel of God" (Acts 20.27) and to constantly be vigilant against false teaching. The churches of Galatia demonstrate to us that false teachings do not just cause problem in young churches—even established and stable churches can be led astray. Let us all strive to continue to hold to the Gospel as originally preached and revealed in the New Testament, lest we become accursed! (Gal 1.6–9).

Philippi

And a vision appeared to Paul in the night: There was a man of Macedonia standing, beseeching him, and saying, "Come over into Macedonia, and help us." (Acts 16.9)

This vision in the night began the evangelization of Europe, which itself began in Philippi. Paul did not stay terribly long, having been forced out by persecution; nevertheless, the seed that had been sown grew and flourished in Philippi, and Paul gained a stalwart supporter of his ministry and the Kingdom in the church in Philippi. Let us consider the church in Philippi, one which constantly comforted and refreshed Paul.

Geography and History

Philippi is a city in northeastern Greece, about 415 miles northeast of Athens and 880 miles northwest of Jerusalem, in the Roman province of Macedonia. It is eight miles inland from its port city, Neapolis (*cf.* Acts 16.11), and sits on the Egnatian Way, one of the arteries of the Roman Empire. Philippi stands in a relatively fertile area, having a river nearby.

Philippi was originally settled as a mining town to exploit the gold fields that lay nearby. After the gold ran out, the city remained on account of its presence on the Egnatian Way. Philip of Macedon in the fourth century BCE fortified the city and named it after himself.

Macedonia became part of the Roman Empire in 168 BCE and was organized as a province twenty years later. After the civil wars in Rome in the first century BCE, Octavian (Augustus) rewarded his soldiers with land near Philippi, and the city was turned into a Roman colony. This afforded its inhabitants full Roman citizenship, and therefore the Philippians were in no mood to tolerate anything that would seem amiss by the Roman authorities. The city was renamed Colonia Julia Augusta Philippensis and was populated mostly by the families of Roman soldiers and their descendants.

Unlike many of the other cities in which Paul preached, Philippi did not contain a large Jewish population; there was no synagogue there to our knowledge, and the small group of Jews present would meet at the river bank on the Sabbath for prayers (*cf.* Acts 16.13). The city was mostly Gentile, and, more specifically, mostly Roman; there were many wealthy Romans within the city, although there did remain a Greek lower class that supported the standard superstitions of the day. Philippi was fully pagan, yet records do not indicate that it was known for any excessive immorality. While the fields were ripe for harvest in Philippi, promoting the Gospel there would not be easy.

The Beginnings of the Church in Philippi

In 49–51, after Paul and Silas visited the churches that Paul had helped to establish previously in Galatia, they and their associates attempted to go and preach in other parts of Asia Minor, but were prevented from doing so by the Holy Spirit (Acts 16.1–8). Having come to Troas, Paul receives the following revelation as recorded in Acts 16.9–10:

> And a vision appeared to Paul in the night: There was a man of Macedonia standing, beseeching him, and saying, "Come over into Macedonia, and help us."
>
> And when he had seen the vision, straightway we sought to go forth into Macedonia, concluding that God had called us to preach the gospel to them.

Incidentally, it would seem that Luke the author is now present with Paul and Silas since the narrative switches to the first person plural.

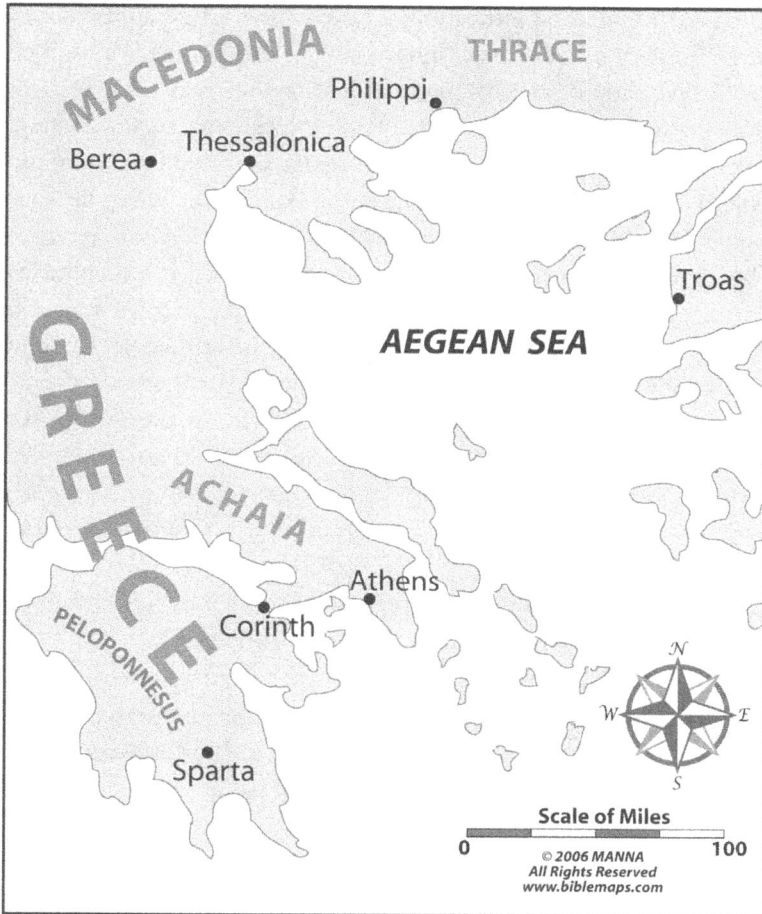

The men sailed to Neapolis and from there proceeded to Philippi (Acts 16.11–12). Paul's regular custom was to enter the synagogue and preach to the Jews (*cf.* Acts 17.1–2). We can conclude, however, that there was no synagogue in Philippi, since Paul and his associates went outside the city to a river area where they supposed that Jews would meet to pray on the Sabbath (Acts 16.13). Lydia was present at this meeting, described as a "seller of purple" from Thyatira in Asia Minor, and was most likely a proselyte or a God-fearer. She was persuaded to obey the Lord Jesus and constrained Paul and his associates to remain in her house (Acts 16.14–15).

Luke provides no indication of exactly how long Paul remained in Philippi save a reference to remaining there "some days" in Acts 16.12. We should not presume that his stay was very long, perhaps only a few weeks. The reason for Paul's quick departure is given in Acts 16.16–40: Paul was being constantly harassed by a slave girl with a spirit of divination, and he commanded the demon to come out of her. Her owners, having lost a source of income, dragged Paul before the authorities and charged him as a Jew advocating practices that Romans should not practice. Paul and Silas were publicly beaten and then thrown into prison; in the middle of the night, while they were praying and singing, a great earthquake occurred and loosed their bonds. These events led to the conversion of the jailer and his household. When the morning came, Paul demanded that the magistrates come to lead him out of prison because his rights as a Roman citizen had been violated; the magistrates did so, apologizing and encouraging Paul and Silas to leave. They departed from Philippi, although Luke seems to have been left behind, since the first person plural narrative ends after Acts 16.19.

The church in Philippi thus began with Paul's preaching for a brief time and the continued ministry of Luke and perhaps some others. It is quite likely that the Philippian brethren continued to suffer some persecution at the hands of the Roman authorities and/or citizens of Philippi; nevertheless, as we shall see, they remained faithful to the Lord.

The Church in Philippi, 52–155 CE

Paul found opportunities to return to Philippi after his original preaching trip there. It would seem that at some point during his time in Ephesus, somewhere between 55–57 CE, Paul went to Macedonia intending to find Titus; while the text does not indicate precisely where Paul visited within Macedonia, it is highly likely that he spent at least some time in Philippi (2 Cor 2.13; 7.5). Paul also intended to travel again to Macedonia after his two years in Ephesus around 57 and was able to do so (Acts 19.21; 20.1). He returned again to Asia Minor through Macedonia, and Philippi is mentioned specifically in this context (Acts 20.3–6).

Paul is believed to have written his letter to the Philippians during his first Roman imprisonment, *ca.* 60–62 CE (*cf.* Phil 1.12–14; 4.22). After this, Paul seems to have traveled again among the churches, and from 1 Timothy 1.3 it seems that Paul departed from Ephesus to Macedonia, likely visiting Philippi again around 63–64. We have no other recorded visits of Paul to Philippi or Macedonia. In sum, Paul visited the brethren in Philippi again about four times between 52 and 64.

While the New Testament does not provide any more witness to the church in Philippi, there is some evidence from early Christian literature regarding the state of the church in the early second century. There is a supposed letter of Ignatius of Antioch to the Philippians (d. 115), but it is believed to be spurious by many and datable to the end of the century. Nevertheless, Polycarp of Smyrna wrote an undisputed letter to the church in Philippi sometime between 115 and 155 CE; in it, he established that the brethren there were continuing in their love for one another and in the doctrine which Paul had taught them (Polycarp, *Letter to the Philippians* 1–9) and encouraged them to remain faithful. Polycarp indicated that there was a problem with an elder named Valens who had fallen into covetousness and required repentance (11). Unfortunately, the brethren in Philippi indicated a desire to obtain copies of the letters of Ignatius of Antioch, who is well-known for promoting the idea of having one bishop over a collective of elders in local congregations and who stimulated the progressive apostasy into Catholicism (13). Nevertheless, this evidence demonstrates that the church was still present and strong in the second century.

The Church in Philippi: Supporting Brethren

"I thank my God upon all my remembrance of you, always in every supplication of mine on behalf of you all making my supplication with joy, for your fellowship in furtherance of the gospel from the first day until now" (Phil 1.3–5).

When we consider the New Testament evidence regarding the church in Philippi, we find that a consistent theme is their support of brethren. While it is possible that some of the brethren, like Lydia, were wealthy, it is also possible that the church overall comprised more of the poorer set (*cf.* 2 Cor 8.2). Nevertheless, the amount of money the brethren in Philippi had available is not relevant; the fact that they constantly used it to support their brethren is of great consequence. Paul indicates that the churches of Macedonia and Achaia purposed to give to the church in Jerusalem (Rom 15.23), and he greatly praised the brethren in Macedonia (which would include Philippi) who gave "beyond their means" for this purpose (2 Cor 8.1–5).

The church in Philippi also greatly assisted Paul in his preaching in other places. Paul recalled in Philippians 4.15–16 how the church in Philippi sent him aid while he was in Thessalonica and how they were in fact the only church to do so. He continued by establishing in Philippians 4.18 that he had again received some benefit from Philippi from Epaphroditus. Paul indicated in Philippians 4.10 that the Philippians have always manifested concern for him, but were only able to provide assistance at specific times, and that he recognized as much.

We can see, therefore, that the church in Philippi excelled at assisting brethren, both those preaching the Gospel and those in need, with whatever financial resources they had available to them.

The Church in Philippi: Loving the Brethren

"And this I pray, that your love may abound yet more and more in knowledge and all discernment" (Phil 1.9).

What prompted the brethren in Philippi to be willing to give so generously to those in need? They loved their brethren! Paul speaks of that love as already existing in Philippians 1.9, and it is made manifest in their attitudes toward others and one another.

Paul speaks of Epaphroditus in Philippians 2.25–28; he seems to be either an evangelist or at least someone highly active in the promotion of the Gospel, and he seems to have been sent by the Philippians to Paul during his imprisonment in Rome. Evidently, Epaphroditus became terribly ill, almost to the point of death, and yet he recovered. Paul expects that when they see him that they will rejoice, and we can conclude that since Epaphroditus himself was troubled at hearing that the brethren in Philippi had heard he was ill, that such indicates the great care and concern he knows would exist in Philippi on his behalf on account of his condition.

It is also clear how the Philippians loved Paul and the work which Paul did in the Kingdom by their continual support and concern and obedience to that which he taught them (*cf.* Phil 4.10–18; 2.12). Similarly, Paul makes his love for them known (Phil 4.1). Despite the suffering and humiliation he received in Philippi and the chains in which he currently found himself, the love and example of the brethren in Philippi gave him great encouragement in his work in the Kingdom (1 Thes 2.2; Phil 1). Paul was not able to say such things about every church!

The Church in Philippi: Standing Firm

"So then, my beloved, even as ye have always obeyed, not as in my presence only, but now much more in my absence, work out your own salvation with fear and trembling" (Phil 2.12).

The love shared by the brethren in Philippi for each other and for Paul naturally led them to stand firm for the truth and the doctrines in which Paul instructed them. Of all the "personalized" letters of Paul to churches, Philippi appears to have had the fewest problems. In Philippians 4.2, Paul exhorts Euodia and Syntyche to "be of the same mind in the Lord," and in Philippians 4.3 he encourages Syzygus (or perhaps "true yokefellow," another individual in Philippi) to help them work together. Whatever matter prompted this statement is unknown, but it represents the only definite difficulty found within the church in Philippi. Perhaps there was some disagreement regarding how to strive for growth in Christ Jesus based on Philippians 3.15, but that is not entirely clear. Paul does spend some time encouraging the brethren to be on the lookout for error, be it through "Judaizers" (Phil 3.2) or false teachers (Phil 3.18–19); there is no indication, however, that such was causing difficulty in Philippi at that time.

Paul provides excellent instruction within the letter to the Philippians; it would seem, however, that this instruction is by way of reminder and encouragement (Phil 2.12; 3.1), and not a sign of actual problems in Philippi regarding these matters.

We should note that there were elders and deacons in Philippi when Paul wrote to them (Phil 1.1); this may provide some of the explanation for the peace within the Philippian church. Nevertheless, Paul encourages the brethren to greater unity and concern for others, as evidenced in Philippians 2.1–11. Paul constantly encourages them to maintain and develop greater obedience to God (Phil 1.9–10; 1.27; 2.12–16; 4.9). Perhaps one of the most excellent summations of this is found in Philippians 3.8–15a:

> Yea verily, and I count all things to be loss for the excellency of the knowledge of Christ Jesus my Lord: for whom I suffered the loss of all things, and do count them but refuse, that I may gain Christ, and be found in him, not having a righteousness of mine own, even that which is of the law, but that which is through faith in Christ, the righteousness which is from God by faith: that I may know him, and the power of his resurrection, and the fellowship of his sufferings, becoming conformed unto his death; if by any means I may attain unto the resurrection from the dead. Not that I have already obtained, or am already made perfect: but I press on, if so be that I may lay hold on that for which also I was laid hold on by Christ Jesus. Brethren, I could not myself yet to have laid hold: but one thing I do, forgetting the things which are behind, and stretching forward to the things which are before, I press on toward the goal unto the prize of the high calling of God in Christ Jesus. Let us therefore, as many as are perfect, be thus minded.

Paul also encourages the brethren to remember that their citizenship is in Heaven, not on earth (Phil 3.20), and to continually focus on that which is positive and edifying in the faith (Phil 4.8). Furthermore, a continual theme in Philippians is the need to rejoice in the Lord; Paul, in effect, commands this three times (Phil 3.1; 4.4), and this seems to have not been burdensome for the brethren in Philippi.

Conclusion

"Even as it is right for me to be thus minded on behalf of you all, because I have you in my heart, inasmuch as, both in my bonds and in the defence and confirmation of the gospel, ye all are partakers with me of grace" (Phil 1.7).

Where do encouragers get their encouragement? This has been the question that has often bedeviled evangelists for years. Churches that serve as encouragement for encouragers have a special place in God's plan, and Philippi most certainly served that function for Paul. The church in Philippi began quickly and under duress, and yet the brethren remained firm in the faith through the love of God and the brethren. From the beginning they worked to help brethren in times of need, and constantly refreshed the spirit of Paul. The church in Philippi was stable, shepherded by elders and served by deacons, and perhaps had greater peace than any other New Testament church. The church in Philippi thus stands as an excellent example for us of a strong church that provides encouragement to so many within its fold and within the Kingdom at large, and that churches can be at peace, sharing the love of the brethren, standing firm for the truth, and working to promote the Gospel locally and abroad. Let us be encouraged by Philippi to ourselves be strong enough to encourage the encouragers, and receive commendation from God!

Thessalonica

And ye became imitators of us, and of the Lord, having received the
word in much affliction, with joy of the Holy Spirit; so that ye became
an ensample to all that believe in Macedonia and in Achaia.
(1 Thes 1.6–7)

Everything stood against the success of the Gospel in Thessalonica. Located in a prosperous, worldly city filled with not only paganism but also zealous Jews, the church in Thessalonica saw Paul for only a short amount of time and endured great persecution. Far from destroying their faith, however, the persecution strengthened and matured the church in Thessalonica, and Thessalonica, like Philippi, was one of Paul's encouraging churches.

Geography and History
Thessalonica (modern Saloniki) is located in Greece on the north end of the Gulf of Salonika. The capital of the Roman province of Macedonia, Thessalonica is 73 miles directly southwest of Philippi, although it is around 100 miles by the Egnatian Way; the city is also about 185 miles northeast of Athens and 915 miles northwest of Jerusalem.

Thessalonica was a port city, located on a rich and well-watered plain on the Egnatian Way, one of the main arteries of the Roman Empire. Its presence on that road as a port city (the first port city on the Aegean Sea, if coming from the west) led to its great population and prosperity. In Paul's day the city had about 200,000 people and was very rich on account of its trade. People would enter in and depart from Thessalonica, engaging in trade;

the city was rather cosmopolitan and highly connected to the rest of the Roman world (*cf.* 1 Thes 1.8–9).

The city was founded in 316 BCE by Cassander, one of the generals of Alexander the Great; he named it after his wife, who happened to also be the sister of Alexander. Thessalonica was by far the greatest city in Macedonia and was full of the paganism of the day. In all likelihood there was a Jewish neighborhood in Thessalonica, for the Jewish population was fairly significant and wielded some influence over the city as a whole (*cf.* Acts 17.5). While Philippi was a Roman colony, full of Roman soldiers, and therefore conservative and peaceful, Thessalonica was a bustling, cosmopolitan, commercial center. Nevertheless, the Gospel took hold in this land, as we shall see.

The Founding of the Church in Thessalonica, 50–51 CE

After the beating and suffering endured in Philippi (*cf.* Acts 16; 1 Thes 2.2), Paul traveled and passed through Amphipolis and Apollonia (Acts 17.1); no mention is made, however, of any evangelistic work done in that area. After this Paul arrived in Thessalonica, and as was his custom, he entered the synagogue and began demonstrating to the Jews there that Jesus was the Christ (Acts 17.2–3). Luke informs us that many of the Jews believed, along with many of the Greek proselytes or "God-fearers" and many of the leading women (Acts 17.4).

Nevertheless, many other Jews became jealous and, having incited the city, led forth many of the brethren before the city rulers. They claimed that the brethren had "turned the world upside down" and that they were teaching disobedience to Caesar by preaching Jesus as King (Acts 17.5–7). These claims troubled the city rulers; nevertheless, after receiving some money, the authorities let the brethren go, and they sent Paul and Silas to Berea by night (Acts 17.8–10).

How long was Paul in Thessalonica? Luke indicates that he reasoned with the Jews in the synagogue for three Sabbaths (Acts 17.2). This would indicate a timeframe between two and a half weeks to about four weeks. Many allege, however, that this was

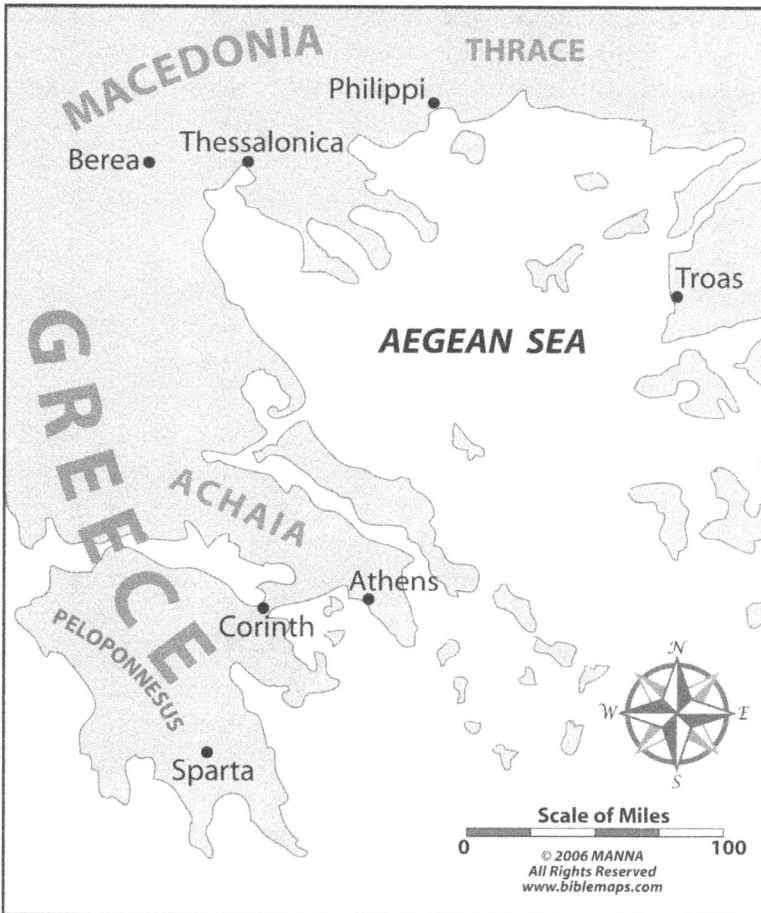

not enough time for Paul to have been in Thessalonica. It is believed that Paul was employed in Thessalonica in 1 Thessalonians
2.9 and 2 Thessalonians 3.7–9 and that he received two aid pack-
ages from Philippi while in Thessalonica (Phil 4.15–16). It is also
believed that four weeks was not enough time for Paul to teach
the Thessalonians. Regardless, we see in Acts 18.1–5 that Paul
immediately found work in Corinth when he was there and that
when his fellow laborers returned he immediately set to preaching the Gospel full-time; such a scenario would be possible also
in Thessalonica. The very fact that Luke provides a rather specific

timeframe is significant and should not be so easily brushed aside. The overall chronology of the second missionary journey also lends credence to the view that Paul spent only a short time in Thessalonica. It is reasonable for us to conclude, therefore, that Paul was in Thessalonica anywhere between three weeks and two months.

Paul and the Thessalonians

Paul realized that he left the church there in difficult straits, and he was clearly very concerned about their welfare. When he was in Athens not long after his time in Berea, Paul felt compelled to send Timothy back to Thessalonica to inquire of their condition and was overjoyed when he heard that things were well (*cf.* 1 Thes 3.1–10). As a result of Timothy's report, Paul wrote 1 Thessalonians from Corinth, probably in 51 CE, and it was very possibly the first book of the New Testament to be written. A few months to a year later, Paul wrote 2 Thessalonians to the brethren in Thessalonica, having received further news of their conduct and welfare by letter or by a messenger.

The rest of the recorded interaction between Paul and the Thessalonians correlates to the interaction between Paul and the Philippians. His probable visit to Macedonia during his stay in Ephesus between 55–57 likely included a stay in Thessalonica (2 Cor 2.13; 7.5); he also likely visited Thessalonica once or twice in 57 after his time in Ephesus and before he went to Jerusalem (Acts 19.21; 20.1; 20.3–6). Likewise, his post-imprisonment visit to Macedonia around 63–64 as recorded in 1 Timothy 1.3 probably also included some time in Thessalonica. No other visits are recorded in the Scriptures; we can see, therefore, that Paul probably visited Thessalonica again another three or four times after the church there was established.

The Church in Thessalonica: The Crucible of Persecution

To say that the church in Thessalonica began under difficult circumstances would be an understatement. Paul had only been in Thessalonica for a few weeks when persecution arose against the church, but this time Paul and Silas did not bear the brunt of the suffering—the brethren themselves did (Acts 17.5–9). The persecution was not just from Jews, but also from the Gentiles; the Thessalonians were suffering similar things from the hands of the Gentiles as did the believers in Judea from the Jews (1 Thes 2.14–16). The brethren were thus suffering persecution for a faith in which they had believed for fewer than three months; it is at once clear why Paul was so concerned for these brethren! He loved them deeply (1 Thes 2.7–8), speaking to them with tender language that he did not use with other churches.

We can only imagine the joy that Paul felt when hearing how the church in Thessalonica stood firmly in the face of such opposition (*cf.* 1 Thes 3.1–10). They not only were surviving in the midst of persecution, but were also growing and being strengthened in the faith:

> So that ye became an ensample to all that believe in Macedonia and in Achaia. For from you hath sounded forth the word of the Lord, not only in Macedonia and Achaia, but in every place your faith to God-ward is gone forth; so that we need not to speak anything. For they themselves report concerning us what manner of entering in we had unto you; and how ye turned unto God from idols, to serve a living and true God, and to wait for his Son from heaven, whom he raised from the dead, even Jesus, who delivereth us from the wrath to come. (1 Thes 1.7–10)

Paul was able to say that the church in Thessalonica was "[his] glory and [his] joy" (1 Thes 2.20) since they had remained so steadfast in the Lord despite the persecution they had suffered.

The situation was no less true a few months later; the brethren still suffered persecution as Paul wrote 2 Thessalonians (2 Thes 1.3–6), and yet they remained steadfast in the faith.

The church in Thessalonica was born in the crucible of persecution and grew strong quickly. The brethren seem to have reached a level of development in the faith after only a few months that eluded Corinth—despite Paul's labors for eighteen months—or even Jerusalem, which shared the Gospel for over 25 years. Persecution did not hinder the church in Thessalonica; instead, it caused the church to grow quickly, advancing far beyond its years.

The Church in Thessalonica: Love and Proper Conduct

We have no reason to doubt that persecution led the brethren in Thessalonica to love each other as God intended (*cf.* 1 Thes 4.9). It no longer mattered whether they were Jewish or Greek, whether they were rich or poor, or any other possible matter of distinction: they were together suffering for the name of Jesus, and they exhorted one another and built one another up by the will of God (1 Thes 5.11). It is little wonder, then, that Paul had no need to write to them to command them to love each other; he simply encouraged them to abound more and more (1 Thes 4.10).

This love, however, was not reserved only for one another; Paul indicates that the love of the Thessalonians extends to all the brethren in Macedonia (1 Thes 4.10). We know that they provided benevolence to Paul and other brethren in need, much like the Philippians: the Thessalonians are part of the "Macedonians" mentioned as providing aid to the needy saints in Jerusalem in Romans 15.23, and doing so beyond their means in 2 Corinthians 8.1–5. It is also likely that some from Thessalonica were part of those who came and brought assistance to Paul while he was in Corinth (2 Cor 11.8–9). While Paul encouraged them to not be weary of well-doing (2 Thes 3.13), he had little to fear.

Likewise, the personal conduct of most of the Thessalonians was properly grounded and established. Paul establishes that the brethren walk according to the example of Paul and those who were with them, and were walking with God and pleasing God (1 Thes 4.1). Paul continues to establish how they avoided sexually deviant behavior, properly possessing themselves in honor, and not wronging their brethren (1 Thes 4.2–8). Paul encourages them to continue to live quiet lives, working to provide for themselves and others, and to walk becomingly before those who were not of the faith (1 Thes 4.11–12; 2 Thes 3.12). They are also to treat those who labor among them for the Gospel well, indicating that there were some evangelists and/or teachers present (1 Thes 5.12–13).

Paul also provides some general instructions and encouragement to the brethren in Thessalonica, encouraging them to be at peace, to admonish the disorderly, to encourage the fainthearted and the weak, and to have patience with all men (1 Thes 5.14–15). The brethren were to rejoice always, to pray without ceasing, and to give thanks to God for all things (1 Thes 5.16–18). The brethren were to furthermore strive not to quench the Spirit, not to despise prophesyings, and to prove all things, holding fast to that which is good and abstaining from that which is evil (1 Thes 5.19–22). We have every reason to believe that the Thessalonians stood firm in these matters.

The brethren in Thessalonica thus walked according to their profession, loving one another in the faith, doing good to those in need, and living according to the commands of God. We can fully understand why Paul loved the brethren in Thessalonica so deeply.

Eschatology in Thessalonica

While things were good overall in Thessalonica, there was one matter that caused concern among the brethren: eschatology. It should not surprise us that the brethren in Thessalonica looked toward the end of the age and the return of Jesus; in times of suffering and persecution, Christians often look forward to the upcoming judgment and vindication of the saints; such is precisely Paul's message in 2 Thessalonians 1.6–10.

First Thessalonians indicates that some of the brethren were concerned about the nature of the resurrection. They were concerned that those who died would not be able to attain to the resurrection of the body (1 Thes 4.13). Paul tries to comfort them, indicating that the dead in Christ shall arise first, and then those who are alive will follow (1 Thes 4.14–17). The brethren were to take comfort in this (1 Thes 4.18).

It is manifest that Paul taught the Thessalonians about the return of Jesus while he was with them, for in his letter to them he indicates that they knew well the nature of the Lord's return, how it would come quickly and when not expected by many (1 Thes 5.1–3). He then encourages the brethren to remain vigilant, to be aware that the end could come at any time, and therefore to live always in obedience to God (1 Thes 5.4–10). He also taught them regarding the events that would occur before the Lord's return, and reminds them of such in 2 Thessalonians 2.

While we have no reason to doubt that the church in Thessalonica openly received the first letter Paul sent to them and took comfort in its message, difficulties in regards to matters of eschatology did not go away. Apparently some had preached or taught, either in person or by a letter pretending to be from Paul, that the day of the Lord was imminent, which disturbed the brethren (2 Thes 2.1–2). Paul reassured them that certain things had to first occur, and encouraged them to not be shaken in their faith (2 Thes 2.3–17).

More disconcerting, however, was the fact that some of the brethren in Thessalonica quit whatever job they worked and lived idly, expecting the Lord to come at any time to deliver them (2 Thes 3.11). This situation could not be tolerated: such persons were charged to work in quietness and eat their own bread, and that if they were not to work, they should not eat (2 Thes 3.10–12). Furthermore, Paul instructs the brethren to withdraw themselves from and to have no company with anyone who walks disorderly and does not follow the commands and traditions which he had delivered to them (2 Thes 3.6, 14). Such persons were not to be considered enemies, however, but ought to be warned as brothers (2 Thes 3.15).

The matter of eschatology thus provided some difficulties and conflicts for the church in Thessalonica. While it is never revealed explicitly how the situation turned out, we can have all confidence that the brethren remained steadfast in their hope, waiting for the day of the Lord and living quietly in the meantime.

Conclusion

While persecution and suffering are never pleasant, Christians who endure them tend to be stronger in the faith. Nowhere was this made more evident than in Thessalonica: a church that had existed for barely a month or two was called upon to persevere through the trials of persecution, and yet the brethren remained steadfast and were strengthened. The church in Thessalonica demonstrates to us that maturity and strength do not just belong to older, more established churches; persecution can refine the character of Christians rather quickly, and the faith of the brethren in Thessalonica puts brethren in other churches to shame.

Since the brethren in Thessalonica suffered for the name of Jesus, they took their commitment to His path seriously. Their love for one another was unquestioned; their conduct was becoming of their profession, and therefore the witness of their faith sounded out through Macedonia and Achaia to the whole world. There were some matters of difficulty, especially in terms of eschatology, but they worked through those on account of the strong faith and commitment of the brethren to Christ and one another.

While most churches today do not suffer persecution as the church in Thessalonica did, their witness can still comfort and encourage. The faith can survive anything that is thrown at it, and faith can even be made stronger in times of difficulty and duress (*cf.* Jas 1.2–4; 1 Pet 1). A church can be mature and yet simultaneously need encouragement in order to grow. The church in Thessalonica demonstrates clearly that a committed group of Christians who survive the crucible of this world can provide a beacon of faith that can spread throughout the whole world and be an encouragement to many.

Corinth

Paul, called to be an apostle of Jesus Christ through the will of God, and Sosthenes our brother, unto the church of God which is at Corinth, even them that are sanctified in Christ Jesus, called to be saints, with all that call upon the name of our Lord Jesus Christ in every place, their Lord and ours. (1 Cor 1.1–2)

Corinth. In the ancient world, the place was synonymous with immorality and excess. The city of Corinth had the same reputation in the ancient world as Las Vegas has today for Americans—"what happens here stays here"—and sin was prevalent everywhere. The Gospel took root in Corinth with great difficulty, although not as it had in Macedonia. The difficulties in Corinth were mostly internal: strife, division, dissension, immorality, unfaithfulness, and the list can go on and on—so much so that it is a marvel that Paul calls them "saints"! The church in Corinth, as we shall see, was a "problem" church, and Paul and others put great effort into exhorting and rebuking the brethren there.

Geography and History

Corinth is located in modern Greece, the capital of the ancient Roman province of Achaia, 56 miles west of Athens, 180 miles southwest of Thessalonica, and about 815 miles northwest of Jerusalem. Corinth's unique position led to its prosperity; it sits on an isthmus joining the Peloponnesus to mainland Greece. The acrocorinth, the main acropolis of the city, sat 1,886 feet above sea level, and was easily defended. Any land traffic traveling north or south through Greece would pass through Corinth. Corinth also controlled two ports: Cenchreae in the east, on the Aegean Sea; and Lechaeum in the west, on the Gulf of Corinth, which led to the Ionian Sea. Most commercial ships of the day chose to transport their cargo across the isthmus than to brave the seas around the Peloponnesus. Corinth, therefore, became a major commercial hub of the Roman Empire, totaling 300,000 citizens and 460,000 slaves and plenty of wealth.

Corinth was founded during the ninth century BCE and grew into a prosperous Greek city-state, often allied with other Peloponnesian states. It became part of the Roman Empire in the second century BCE, but was razed to the ground after rebelling against Rome in 146 BCE. Nevertheless, Julius Caesar rebuilt the city in 46 BCE, and it quickly grew again to great size and prominence.

Corinth was mostly known as a pleasure city. Its quick rise to wealth, its transient population, and the freedom to participate in licentious behavior joined together to create a city known for its immorality. The phrase, "to live like a Corinthian," meant to live a life of sexual indulgence and drunkenness. Corinth was home to a large temple to Aphrodite (Latin Venus), the goddess of love; before the destruction of 146 BCE, that temple employed 1,000 temple prostitutes and was still prevalent afterward.

Corinth, therefore, was in dire need of the Gospel message. Would its inhabitants hear the message?

The Founding of the Church in Corinth, 50–52 CE

After Paul's quick departure from Thessalonica, he traveled first to Berea and then on to Athens (Acts 17.10–15). Paul did some preaching in Athens; while some converted, the preaching of the Gospel there was not very fruitful, and Paul soon moved on to Corinth, where he waited for some of his associates who were still in Macedonia (Acts 17.16–18.1). He soon found Aquila and Priscilla (or Prisca), Jews originally from Asia Minor who were evicted from Rome. Since they were tentmakers like Paul, Paul lived and worked with them (and evidently converted them: Acts 18.18, 24–28). He was also preaching in the synagogue, and many Jews and Greeks believed (Acts 18.1–4).

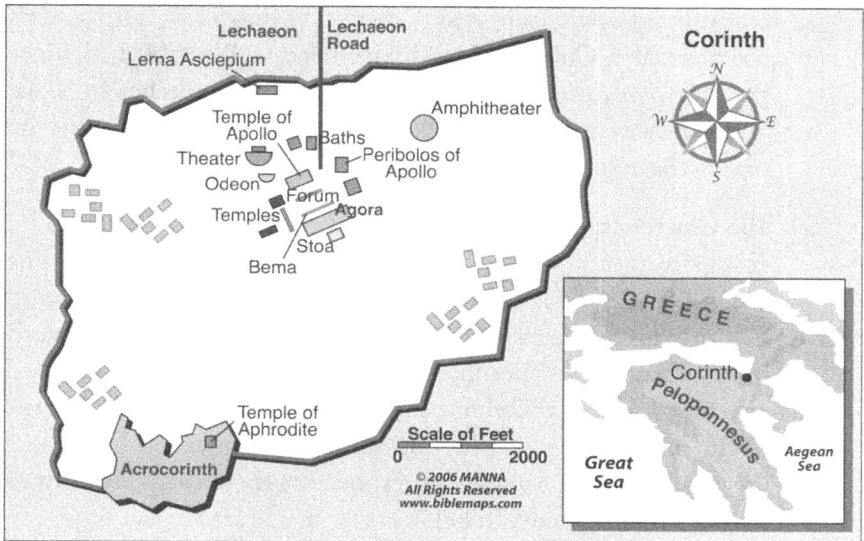

When Silas and Timothy arrived from Macedonia, Paul began preaching in earnest and remained in Corinth for eighteen months (Acts 18.5, 11). When the Jews would no longer hear, Paul began staying with a believer, Titius Justus, whose house was next to the synagogue. He kept teaching, converting even Crispus the leader of the synagogue (Acts 18.6–8). Jesus even appeared to Paul in a dream, establishing that He had "many people" in Corinth (Acts 18.9–11).

His preaching continued until the Jews brought charges against him before Gallio the proconsul of Achaia (Acts 18.12–14). Gallio, however, would have none of it, telling the Jews to deal with their own squabbles (Acts 18.14–16). The new leader of the synagogue, Sosthenes, was then dragged out and beaten (Acts 18.17). (It is not known whether Sosthenes was a Christian and beaten by Jews or if he was beaten by the Greeks because of the tumult raised by the Jews.) Disturbed by this turn of events, Paul soon took his leave of Corinth, sailing off to Ephesus with Aquila and Priscilla (Acts 18.18).

Historical information allows us to place Gallio in Corinth in 51–52 CE; depending on the precise timeframe, Paul was in

Corinth anywhere from mid 50 to mid 51 into 52. By all accounts, the church in Corinth should have been well-established, since Paul was with them far longer than with the churches in Macedonia; however, future events demonstrate that such was by no means the case.

The Church in Corinth, 52–100 CE

Things were not well in Corinth. A few years later, sometime around 55–56, as Paul is in Ephesus (Acts 19), a delegation of Corinthians arrives with a letter from the brethren there regarding marriage and other matters (1 Cor 7.11; 16.8, 17). Paul had also heard from certain brethren of Chloe's house regarding many of the problems present in Corinth (1 Cor 1.11), and he wrote 1 Corinthians from Ephesus in response to these many difficulties (discussed in more depth below).

We cannot know precisely how effective the first letter to the Corinthians turned out. Paul apparently visited Corinth soon after sending 1 Corinthians and rebuked and exhorted the brethren (*ca.* 55–57; 2 Cor 13.1). Such was not taken very well by them (2 Cor 12.19–13.2). Meanwhile, certain men carrying commendation from some Jewish source went into Corinth and attempted to persuade the brethren to listen to them and not to Paul; it is very likely that these were some "Judaizing" teachers (2 Cor 10.12; 11.2–4, 11–23). Suffering some distresses in Ephesus, Paul sent Titus to address the situation (2 Cor 1.8–10; 7.13–14). After he escaped from Asia, Paul met up with Titus in Macedonia (2 Cor 2.12–13). Having received Titus' report, he wrote the second letter to the Corinthians from Macedonia to Corinth to address the situation as it stood, intending to visit them very soon to handle the matters in person (*ca.* 57 CE; 2 Cor 13.1–2). Paul indeed visited the brethren in Corinth, no doubt strongly rebuking those in sin and exhorting the brethren to stand firm (Acts 20.2).

After Paul's imprisonment in Rome from 60–62 CE, it is likely that he visited Corinth again after visiting Macedonia, noting that Erastus remained there (*ca.* 63–64; 1 Tim 1.3; 2 Tim 4.20). This is all the New Testament reveals concerning Corinth.

We do have a letter from the church in Rome written to the church in Corinth, dated anywhere from 65–100 CE, believed to have been written by Paul's associate Clement (Phil 4.3) and called 1 Clement. Clement indicates that there were elders in Corinth, but that many had caused division and dissension within the church and had revolted from the leadership of the elders (1 Clement 1, 45–47). While Clement praises the Corinthians for previous obedience and faithfulness (1 Clement 2), he chides the church strongly for their current state, considering it even worse than the problems that prompted 1 and 2 Corinthians (1 Clement 47). The church in Corinth had a reputation for contentiousness and for being zealous about inconsequential matters (1 Clement 45). Clement calls the church to repent, to be humble, and to seek peace, and for those who are guilty of rebellion, to confess and repent (1 Clement 14, 19, 51, 56).

We can see clearly then that the church in Corinth maintained a stormy history, full of all kinds of sin leading to no end of difficulty. This was true during the time of the apostles and even afterward. Let us consider the difficulties this church suffered so that we may not stumble by doing the same.

Problems in Corinth

The problems in Corinth were numerous and severe. Let us try to consider most of them by category.

One of the difficulties that prompted Paul's first letter to the Corinthians was the matter of division and factions among the brethren in Corinth. The church was divided on the basis of loyalties and by socioeconomic status; people identified themselves by a popular evangelist (Paul, Apollos, Cephas) or by Christ, and they made a mockery of the Lord's Supper by observing socioeconomic distinctions (*cf.* 1 Cor 1.11–12; 11.17–34). Such divisiveness indicated to Paul that the brethren in Corinth were still worldly (or carnal), not yet truly spiritual (1 Cor 3.1–4), and that such worldliness provided the overall cause for the many difficulties present in Corinth.

This worldliness often manifested itself in pride, strife, and jealousy, fully condemned in 1 Corinthians 3.18–4.21. When a man took his father's wife, the Corinthians did not mourn, but were puffed up in their "tolerance" (1 Cor 5.1–2). They freely took each other to court in Corinth, accepting the judgment of unbelievers, defrauding one another (1 Cor 6.1–8). They abused their liberty of eating meat sacrificed to idols, being puffed up by knowledge without being tempered by love (1 Cor 8). Not liking Paul's judgmental attitude, the Corinthians turned to teachers who were more amenable, compelling Paul to defend himself in his weaknesses (2 Cor 10–12). Lack of repentance—both of the church with the man of 1 Corinthians 5, and those who persisted in sin despite Paul's earlier rebuke in 2 Corinthians 12.19-13.2—was a most grievous matter, that in some measure required disassociation (1 Cor 5).

Paul and his life in the Gospel was a constant source of dissension and disputation. While some would join a "Paul faction" in Corinth (1 Cor 1.12–15), Paul and his actions were constantly questioned by many. Paul felt compelled to defend his liberties to take a wife and to be paid for preaching (even if not exercised; 1 Cor 9.1–12). The fact that Paul did not receive payment from the Corinthians while working there was even used against him, much to his chagrin (2 Cor 11.7–9; 12.11–13). Despite founding the church with apostolic signs and wonders, Paul felt compelled to defend his ministry against those who glorified and commended themselves against him (2 Cor 10–12); we can only hope that the Corinthians heeded him and repented.

The list does not end there. Paul must exhort the brethren to avoid sexual immorality, particularly involving prostitutes (1 Cor 6.9–20). There were some in Corinth who even advocated that Jesus was not raised from the dead, undermining the foundation of the Gospel (1 Cor 15.12–19)! The Corinthians are constantly warned about their association with unbelievers: 1 Corinthians 15.33 speaks of how evil companionship corrupts good morals, and 2 Corinthians 6.11–18 urges the brethren not to be unequally yoked with unbelievers. The brethren were to learn from Israel and their difficulties to know to avoid idolatry (1 Cor 10.1–14). Their difficulties even extended into the realm of restoration; apparently the brethren in Corinth needed to be told to receive again one who sought restoration without further berating (2 Cor 2.5–11).

First Corinthians 12–14 indicates how prevalent spiritual gifts were in Corinth, particularly of speaking in tongues and prophecy, and it is clear that such gifts are being abused. While Paul set out the proper use of such gifts in order to establish an orderly assembly, he desired to show them the more excellent way. In the end, 1 Corinthians 13 clearly demonstrates for us the problem in Corinth: they did not have love. They focused on their spiritual gifts, their standing in the world, and on many other factors, but neglected love among themselves. If the brethren loved God as they ought, they would have avoided the immorality so present within the church. If the brethren loved each other as they ought, they would have avoided the jealousy, divisiveness, strife, and other difficulties that plagued them. While the churches in Philippi and Thessalonica cultivated the love of the brethren (Phil 1.9; 1 Thes 4.9–10), Corinth apparently did not. Perhaps, in the end, that made all the difference.

Positives of Corinth

We would be remiss if we did not mention some of the positive attributes the Corinthians had that are spoken of by Paul. Despite all the internal dissension, no actual division of the church seems to have taken place. Paul, having informed them of the need to provide a collection for the saints in need, just as the Galatians and Macedonians were doing (Rom 15.26; 1 Cor 16.1), could later boast that they were ready to provide such a gift (2 Cor 8–9). Despite all their problems, Paul could give thanks to God for them (1 Cor 1.4–9). This helps to show us that even if a church is a problem church, it is still a church and should gain our support, not our disdain.

Conclusion

The church in Corinth was a difficult church in a difficult region. While the church was disappointing in the end, it should not surprise us that a beacon of light in such a sinful city should be beset with storms. Nevertheless, the church in Corinth leaves a sad legacy of worldliness and sin, both during the times of the apostles and also afterward. While there were some strengths and some signs of hope, overall the church in Corinth serves as a warning to us. A worldly church is not pleasing to God, will have no end of trouble from within and without, and will easily accept false teachings to justify itself. Corinth demonstrates to us the power of love in a surprising way. Corinth indicates that a church is not strong because an apostle was there preaching the truth for a long time, because a church suffers little persecution, because it is wealthy, or because many of its members have high social standing. Corinth had all these things and was still miserable. A church is made strong because its members love God and one another, and such was what separated Corinth from Philippi and Thessalonica. Let Corinth demonstrate to us the power of love, and let us always strive to obey God and work with one another!

Ephesus

Wherefore I testify unto you this day, that I am pure from the blood of all men. For I shrank not from declaring unto you the whole counsel of God. (Acts 20.26–27)

In the first century CE, Asia Minor (the modern Turkish peninsula) represented some of the most fertile ground for the Gospel; Ephesus, along with the whole province of Asia, was no exception. Of all of the churches he had a hand in establishing, Paul spent the greatest amount of time in Ephesus. There is much revealed about the church in Ephesus within the Scriptures, perhaps more so than any other local New Testament church, and the information provided likely spans a 40-year period.

Geography and History

Ephesus was the gateway to Asia and was the most major city of the Roman province of Asia in modern-day Turkey. The city was approximately 238 miles east of Corinth, 500 miles west northwest of Antioch of Syria, and 615 miles northwest of Jerusalem. In Paul's day, Ephesus was situated on the mouth of the Cayster River where it emptied into the Aegean Sea; the harbor has since silted up, and the ruins of Ephesus are now land-locked. In its day, however, Ephesus represented a major commercial center: a highway ran east from Ephesus through the highlands of Asia Minor directly to Mesopotamia. Many major caravans coming northwest from Mesopotamia, Persia, and India traveled through Ephesus, just as commerce flowed from many parts of the Mediterranean heading east.

While other cultures had previously inhabited the area, Ephesus was established as an Athenian colony in the eleventh century BCE and represented a great prize for any nearby empire, including the Lydians, Persians, and Macedonians. In 188 BCE, the Romans took control of Ephesus and handed it over to the king of Pergamum. In 133, the city was assigned back to the Romans, who controlled it without much incident through New Testament times.

Ephesus was famous not only for its strategic and political importance, but also for its great temple devoted to the Greek goddess Artemis (Roman Diana). In all likelihood, the temple began around a meteorite that fell to earth and resembled the figure of a woman, probably became associated with a fertility goddess before the Greek invasion and was later identified with Artemis (*cf.* Acts 19.35). The temple was one of the seven wonders of the ancient world; at 360 feet long and 180 feet broad, it truly would have been an impressive sight.

Ephesus, then, was a large commercial center with a religious undertone, very proud of its heritage and prestige. Yet, even in the midst of this pagan climate, the Gospel would prosper.

Paul and the Founding of the Church in Ephesus, 52–57 CE

For reasons unknown to us but known to God, Paul and his associates were forbidden to promote the Gospel in Asia when they were in Asia Minor previously during the second missionary journey (Acts 16.6; *ca.* 49–50 CE). Nevertheless, when Paul left Corinth, he and Aquila and Priscilla traveled to Ephesus (Acts 18.18–19; 52 CE). Paul preached in the synagogues and received a warm reception; however, likely because of his vow (Acts 18.18), he chose not to remain in Ephesus, but instead continued to travel southeast to Caesarea, Antioch of Syria, and then through Galatia and Phrygia (Acts 18.22–23; 53–54 CE). Aquila and Priscilla, however, remained in Ephesus (Acts 18.18); through their work, Apollos of Alexandria, who understood only the baptism of John, was shown the more accurate truth concerning Jesus and believed (Acts 18.24–28). Apollos then traveled to Corinth and worked

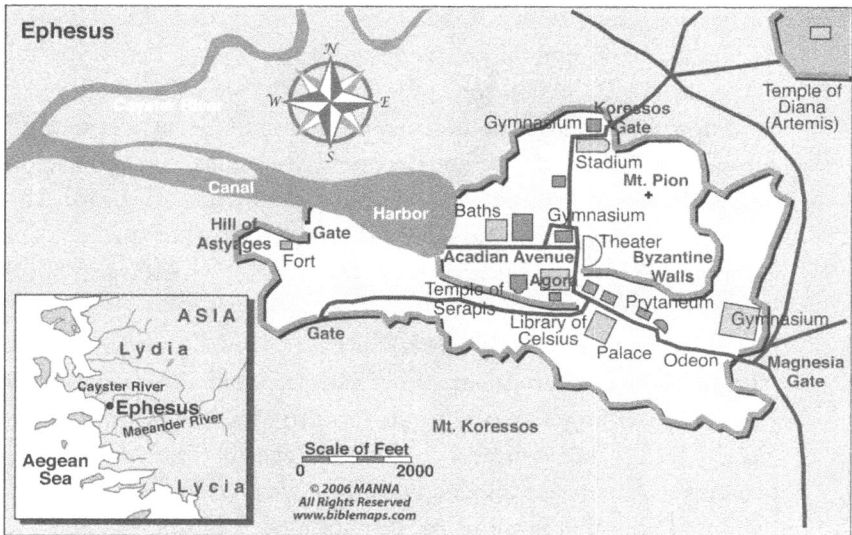

some with the church there; the comment in Acts 18.27 indicates that there were "brethren" in Ephesus, which strongly indicates either that the good work of Paul, Aquila, and Priscilla already bore fruit before Paul worked in Ephesus in earnest or that perhaps some of the Jews who heard and believed on the day of Pentecost had returned back to their native Asia (Acts 2.9, 41).

Paul later returned to Ephesus around 54 CE; he found some disciples of John the Baptist and showed them the truth regarding Jesus and the Holy Spirit, and they believed (Acts 19.1–7). Paul then continued to teach in the synagogue for three months, until the Jews began to revile the Gospel; he then took up residence in the school of Tyrannus and continued to preach (Acts 19.8–9). He did this for two years, and Luke establishes that "all the residents of Asia," Jew and Greek, heard the Word of God (Acts 19.10). Paul's stature in the city is exemplified in his friendship with the Asiarchs, the rulers of Ephesus (Acts 19.31). It was during his stay in Ephesus that Paul wrote 1 Corinthians (1 Cor 16.8, 19), and he likely also visited Corinth at some point during his stay (*cf.* 2 Cor 13.1–2).

Luke provides many episodes that occurred in Ephesus, demonstrating how powerfully the Gospel went forth there. All sorts of diseases and evil spirits were cleansed by God through Paul (Acts 19.11–12). Seven sons of a Jewish high priest named Sceva attempted to cast out demons in the name of "Jesus whom Paul proclaims." When the demon prevailed over them, fear came upon all, and the name of the Lord was magnified (Acts 19.13–16). The sorcerers in town who had believed brought together the books of their magic arts and burned them, the value of which was 50,000 pieces of silver (Acts 19.18–20).

The time had come, however, for Paul to make another journey through Greece, Jerusalem, and finally to Rome; he prepared to depart by sending Timothy and Erastus to Macedonia (Acts 19.21–22; 57 CE). Luke indicates that it was "at this time" that the silversmith Demetrius colluded with his colleagues to incite the city against Paul on account of his promoting the Gospel against the paganism of the day and specifically against the Temple of Artemis (Acts 19.23–27). The cry, "Great is Artemis of the Ephesians!" rose up throughout the city and was centered in the town amphitheater (Acts 19.28–31). The riot (called an *ekklesia,* Acts 19.41) continued for over two hours; finally, the town clerk spoke reasonably and demonstrated that whatever grievances ought to be addressed in the local political assembly (also *ekklesia,* Acts 19.32–41).

Luke indicates that soon after these events, Paul departs for Macedonia (Acts 20.1), likely before his intended time of departure (Pentecost 57; 1 Cor 16.8). Not long after his time in Ephesus he writes to the Corinthians regarding the weighty afflictions that he suffered in Asia, where he despaired even of his life (2 Cor 1.8–10). While some believe that Paul refers there to the events involving Demetrius, it is difficult to correlate the events described in Acts 19.23–41 with the severe description of events in 2 Corinthians 1. Paul indicated in his first Corinthian letter that he "fought with beasts" at Ephesus, and in Acts 20.19 he reminded the Ephesian elders how he suffered trials from the hands of the Jews. When we consider this information, along with the fact that it was the Jews from Asia that began the riot that led to Paul's imprisonment in Jerusalem (*cf.* Acts 21.27–29), we can see that Paul suffered greatly at the hands of the Jews of Asia, likely having been imprisoned and quite near death. This may have happened immediately before or immediately after the riot incited by Demetrius; regardless, this may partly explain Paul's reticence to return to Ephesus on his way to Jerusalem (Acts 20.16) and why he never returned to Ephesus again (Acts 20.25, 38). The church in Ephesus was soundly founded, but many adversaries remained despite the great work done in the city.

Paul and the Ephesians, 58–62

After these events, Paul made his trip through Greece; it is remarked that Tychicus and Trophimus, Asians, are with him (Acts 20.1–4). Paul traveled back through Macedonia to Troas and from there he mostly sails around Asia Minor to Miletus (Acts 20.5–15). Luke records that Paul intentionally sailed past Ephesus since he hoped to make it to Jerusalem by Pentecost (Acts 20.16); nevertheless, he summons the elders of Ephesus to him at Miletus (Acts 20.17). Paul reminded them of his actions and the difficulties that transpired during his time in Ephesus (Acts 20.18–21) and explained to them the things that must suffer (Acts 20.22–23). Paul then revealed to the Ephesian elders that they would never see his face again (Acts 20.24–25), and he declared his innocence of their blood, since he had provided the whole counsel of God (Acts 20.26–27). He then charged them to shepherd the flock of God over which the Holy Spirit made them overseers (Acts 20.28) and warned them of the false teachers and apostasy that would take place, even from some of the very elders themselves (Acts 20.29–31). He then again demonstrated how he had lived among them (Acts 20.32–35), prayed with them (Acts 20.36), and then departed, with the Ephesian elders sorrowful at the prospect of never seeing Paul again (Acts 20.37–38). We have no reason to doubt that Paul's predictions came true.

Nevertheless, the New Testament does contain the letter of Paul to the church in Ephesus (Eph 1.1). It is clear that Paul wrote the letter during his Roman imprisonment (60-62 CE; Eph 6.20); unlike Paul's other letters, however, the one to the

Ephesians is almost entirely bereft of personal information or anecdotes. Paul establishes that he writes to Ephesus (Eph 1.1) and that the aforementioned Tychicus (ostensibly the deliverer of the letter) will inform the brethren of Paul's current state (Eph 6.21–23). The contents of the letter otherwise could have been sent to other churches as well, and it is possible that Paul meant for it to be such an encyclical letter, of which we have the version sent to Ephesus.

Such does not, however, negate the value and importance of the material within the letter to the Ephesians. While Paul goes into great detail regarding the nature of our election in Christ and how God brought the Gentiles into the fold (Eph 1–2) and includes information regarding proper Christian conduct (*cf.* Eph 3–6), we gain the most information about the New Testament church from parts of Ephesians 4 and 5. Much can be learned from Ephesians 4.1–3:

> I therefore, the prisoner in the Lord, beseech you to walk worthily of the calling wherewith ye were called, with all lowliness and meekness, with longsuffering, forbearing one another in love; giving diligence to keep the unity of the Spirit in the bond of peace.

Paul further establishes in Ephesians 4.4–5 that there is one body—that is, one church (*cf.* Col 1.18)—as well as the place of apostles, prophets, evangelists, pastors, and teachers for the building up of that Body, so that it may function and grow properly (Eph 4.11–16). In Ephesians 5.19, Paul demonstrates the need to "speak to one another" in "psalms, hymns, and spiritual songs, singing and making melody with your heart to the Lord."

Ephesians 5.23–33 has long been recognized as a critical passage for understanding God's intention for the marriage relationship, but it also serves as a way of understanding Christ's relationship to the church. The church is to submit to Christ (Eph 5.24). Christ is the head of the church, being its Savior (Eph 5.23–24). Christ loved the church, dying for her, so that those who comprise it could be sanctified, allowing Him to present to Himself a church holy and blameless (Eph 5.25–27). Christ loves the church as He does His own flesh, "for no man ever hated his own flesh" (Eph 5.28–30). Paul then quotes Genesis 2.24—speaking of how a husband and wife leave their parents, join together, and become one flesh—and says that this mystery speaks of Christ and the church (Eph 5.31–32); this can only mean that the church is to leave the world of sin and be joined to Christ so that Christ and the church may become one.

We have no indication that these messages were needed in Ephesus any more than in any other local congregation; any specific correlation to situations in Ephesus would be purely speculative. Nevertheless, we can learn much regarding the proper relationship between members of the church to one another and the relationship of the church to Christ from the material provided by Paul in the Ephesian letter.

Timothy and Ephesus, 63–67

While Paul may not have returned to Ephesus, he did send Timothy to work with the brethren there (1 Tim 1.3). Paul's first letter to Timothy is full of information that likely has many things to do with the church in Ephesus, and also the church overall.

The letter, written around 63–64 CE, includes Paul's encouragement of Timothy to remain in Ephesus to charge certain persons to not teach different doctrines, perhaps partly based on obsessions with stories and genealogies leading to fruitless speculation (1 Tim 1.3–4). Some such persons apparently desired to be teachers, and yet were not fully grounded in the law of Christ, not understanding its true purpose (1 Tim 1.5–11).

Paul then goes on to encourage Timothy to promote prayer and thanksgiving for all men, especially those in authority, so that Christians could live in peace and tranquility (1 Tim 2.1–4). Paul further admonishes Timothy to promote proper roles for men and women (1 Tim 2.8–15). Paul then describes the qualifications for elders, deacons, and their wives (1 Tim 3.1–13); assuming that Ephesus still maintained at least part of the eldership that it had five years previously (*cf.* 1 Tim 5.17–20), the instruction was probably designed to help Timothy know what was expected out of such men or any others whom he would appoint. Paul then indicates his desire to see Timothy soon (whether in Ephesus or somewhere else is not known, nor is whether or not the hope was realized) and that all previous instructions were given so that one may know how one ought to behave in the church, which is established to be the pillar and support of the truth (1 Tim 3.14–15).

Timothy is then told to remind the brethren of the upcoming apostasy predicted by the Spirit and that such apostasy seems to be centered on matters of marriage and food (1 Tim 4.1–6). Timothy is further encouraged to avoid myths and such stories, perhaps akin to those mentioned previously (1 Tim 4.7; *cf.* 1 Tim 1.3–4). Timothy is likewise to provide a good example, exercising toward godliness, which is of more profit than bodily exercise; Paul expects these things to be taught to the brethren (1 Tim 4.4–16).

Paul then explains the type of interaction Christians should have with other brethren in different stages in life (1 Tim 5.1–3) and goes on to speak of widows: the qualifications for enrollment of "widows indeed" to receive support from the church, the exhortation for younger widows to marry, and the principle that family should support widows if family exists, so that the church can focus on those who are "widows indeed" (1 Tim 5.3–16). Paul then speaks of elders: those who rule well should be well-honored (and paid, if it is necessary; 1 Tim 5.17–18). Charges should not be received against elders unless verified by two or three witnesses, and then the elders should be publicly rebuked so that all will fear (1 Tim 5.19–20).

Paul then describes the nature of those who teach falsely (1 Tim 6.3–6) and also provides proper exhortation to those who are rich or who desire to be rich in this world (1 Tim 6.9–10, 17–19). Paul concludes by warning Timothy against the "knowledge" (Greek *gnosis)* that was falsely so-called, by which many swerved in the faith (1 Tim 6.20–21).

From 1 Timothy, then, we get the impression that, overall, things were good in Ephesus, but that there were some who needed to be re-directed back to the truth from fables and stories. Much is said concerning the future and warnings, especially about what would become Gnosticism and other difficulties. Paul's instructions regarding the operation of the church are illuminating and profitable for our understanding of the New Testament church, but it would be speculative to wonder whether there were problems with elders, deacons, widows, or other such things in Ephesus.

A few years later, perhaps around 67 but no later than 68, Paul wrote to Timothy again. The letter makes it clear that Timothy was in Asia (2 Tim 4.19; *cf.* 2 Tim 1.16–18), and it is likely that he remained in Ephesus. Paul knew that he was near death when writing to Timothy, and his letter was very personal (*cf.* 2 Tim 4.6–8).

We can, however, learn some things about the church particularly about the church in Asia. Paul indicates that Christians from Asia "turned away" from him, specifically mentioning Phygelus and Hermogenes (2 Tim 1.15). It is unlikely that Paul was referring to all of the Christians in the province of Asia; it is more likely that he was referring to those Christians from Asia who were in Rome or who traveled in the Roman vicinity. Special mention is made of the house of Onesiphorus, who found Paul and refreshed him (2 Tim 1.16–17). Paul says that Timothy "knows well" how Onesiphorus ministered to them in Ephesus in regards to many things (2 Tim 1.18). Paul provided a touching testimony to the hard work of some of the brethren in Ephesus.

Paul encourages Timothy to entrust what he heard from Paul to many witnesses so that they would also teach it (2 Tim 2.2), and this would be realized in Ephesus. Paul again encourages Timothy to remind the brethren not to strive in matters of words to no profit; the brethren were also to be reminded that they would only be saved if they lived according to the pattern of Christ (2 Tim 2.11–14). Paul again emphasizes the need to "shun profane babblings," remarking in particular about Hymenaeus and Philetus, who taught that the resurrection was already past; this perhaps represents some proto-Gnostic teachings, either in Ephesus or Rome or both (2 Tim 2.16–18).

Paul later speaks about the future condition of many within the church, how they will no longer desire to endure sound teaching but will find teachers of their own desire, turning aside to myth (2 Tim 4.1–4); Timothy is encouraged to remain steadfast and to keep teaching the truth (2 Tim 4.5). Paul also mentions in 2 Timothy 4.12 that he has sent Tychicus to Ephesus; perhaps he is to relieve Timothy, so that the latter may make it to Rome by winter (2 Tim 4.9, 21).

Soon after writing 2 Timothy, Paul meets the end of his earthly life, either in prison or by execution. If indeed Timothy remained in Ephesus, we see that the situation there changed little from before: many needed to return to the truth and to avoid myths and fables, and the prospects for the future included much that was grim.

Around the same time as Paul's first letter to Timothy, Peter wrote 1 Peter to the Christians throughout Asia Minor, which would include Ephesus within the province of Asia (1 Pet 1.1). It is likely, therefore, that the church in Ephesus was suffering some persecution during the 60s (1 Pet 1.6). The rest of the letter, while providing excellent general instruction, does not provide much detail as to the situation in Asia Minor, as established previously with the churches in Galatia.

John and Ephesus, 90s

The final New Testament witness to the church in Ephesus is found in John the Apostle in the book of Revelation. Ephesus is the first of the seven churches of Asia concerning which Jesus provides instruction in Revelation 2.1–7. It is believed that John spent much time working with the church in Ephesus (Eusebius, *History of the Church* 3.1.1) and lived out the rest of his life there (*ibid.*, 3.23.1-5).

Many wish to date the Revelation to the 60s and have it refer to the destruction of Jerusalem. While the book itself provides no date, there are many pieces of evidence that make this view unlikely. Second-century Christian witness unanimously considers the persecution spoken in Revelation 1.9 as coming from Domitian, not Nero, and therefore is between 84–96 CE, with 90–96 CE representing the more likely timeframe (Eusebius, *ibid.*,

3.18.1–4; Irenaeus, *Against Heresies*, 5.30.13). While some may want to cast aspersions on the witness of the early Christians, why they would desire to make the age of Revelation younger and not older is hard to explain. Furthermore, a twenty-five-year gap (or more) between Timothy and the Revelation would nicely explain why Paul never mentions John in Ephesians or 1 and 2 Timothy (or, for that matter, why 1 Timothy would need to be written if John were with Timothy in Ephesus) and why John never mentions Paul or Timothy in any of his letters or Revelation; a two- or three-year gap, if even that long, is much harder to explain. We will proceed, therefore, under the view that John wrote the Revelation from exile in Patmos to the churches of Asia sometime between 90–96 CE.

Jesus Christ, through John, commends the church in Ephesus for many things. The brethren are commended for their work, patience, and endurance, and for having tested false apostles and recognized their deceptiveness (Rev 2.1–3). In these terms, at least, the church followed the instructions of Paul through Timothy as recorded in 1 and 2 Timothy. The church is also commended for hating the "works of the Nicolaitans," hated also by Jesus (Rev 2.6). The New Testament reveals nothing about the Nicolaitans; all that we know about them comes from Clement of Alexandria in the second century and Eusebius of Caesarea in the fourth century. Eusebius establishes that this group lasted only a short time and derived their name from Nicolaus, one of the seven appointed men of Acts 6.5 (Eusebius, *History of the Church* 3.29.1). Eusebius then quotes Clement of Alexandria, who established that the Nicolaitans claimed that Nicolaus had a beautiful wife and since many were jealous of him, he offered her up to any who would marry her; therefore, the Nicolaitans committed sexually deviant behavior with one another's wives without shame (Eusebius, *ibid.*, 3.29.2–3; Clement of Alexandria, *Miscellanies*, 3.4). If the stories as presented by Clement and Eusebius are correct, we can certainly understand why the works of the Nicolaitans were detestable, and it is good that the Ephesians avoided them.

Despite all the good that the church in Ephesus had done, Jesus had something against them: they had left their first love (Rev 2.4). Even though they were doctrinally correct and maintained the truth, the fire had gone out in Ephesus, and the church was not as enamored for the things of Christ as they had been previously. The situation is very grave: if the Ephesians did not repent, the Lord would "remove their candlestick" (Rev 2.5). The church would lose its standing, and the members were in danger of losing their own souls!

Thus the church in Ephesus was mixed by the end of the first century: they withstood heresy and remained patient and steadfast, but their passion had died, and they stood in risk of condemnation. The brethren were encouraged to look back to the earlier days, some perhaps even to the days when Paul was present in Acts 19, and to return to that faith and those works.

In about 115, Ignatius, "bishop" of Antioch, probably wrote a letter to the Ephesians. A shorter and a longer version of this letter remain today; some scholars believe that there are later interpolations even in the shorter version. Regardless, Ignatius speaks of the "bishop" of Ephesus, one Onesimus, along with the "presbytery," indicating that soon after the death of John, the Ephesian church was overtaken by the "one bishop over a plurality of elders" doctrine. Fortunately, it would seem that there were many who did not approve of such things (Ignatius, *Letter to the Ephesians*, 1–2, 3–7, 30). Ignatius warned the Ephesians regarding the prevalent Gnostic heresy, but recognized that the members there have so far rejected them (*ibid*, 8–10, 17). We can see, therefore, how the church in Ephesus was caught up in the beginning of the apostasy in regards to leadership as manifested in the second century, just as Paul had predicted (Acts 20.29–31).

Conclusion

The church in Ephesus represented a prominent church; as we have seen, the Scriptures provide a copious amount of information regarding its existence over a 40-year span. Just as Ephesus was an important and prominent city, so also the church in it was important and prominent. Throughout the Apostolic age the church in Ephesus overall stood firm, although many required rebuke for false teachings.

While the church in Ephesus represents a good example of how a church endures over time, its story is tragic in the end: Jesus must warn it to return to the way it was in earlier days lest they lose their place and souls be lost, and the second-century evidence indicates how the church followed along with the general apostasy that first involved the leadership, providing a sad testimony to Paul's warning. The church in Ephesus was to continue as it had begun, a group of committed disciples standing for the truth of God despite the plots of the Jews and the dangers of the Gentiles, zealous for the things of Christ. Unfortunately, the passion died and subsequently the church lost its hold on the truth. Let us strive to be as what God desired from Ephesus and not turn out as Ephesus.

Rome

And the night following the Lord stood by him, and said, "Be of good cheer: for as thou hast testified concerning me at Jerusalem, so must thou bear witness also at Rome." (Acts 23.11)

Rome—the prize. During New Testament times, Rome was the center of the known world and the capital of the greatest empire known to that time. All roads and shipping lanes led to Rome. With about a million residents, Rome was a vast city, the major commercial and political center of the day. Every belief, superstition, and idea ended up in Rome, and Paul greatly desired to preach the Gospel there both to citizens and to the rulers.

Geography and History

Rome was founded on the Italian peninsula on seven hills around the Tiber River, about 15 miles inland from the Mediterranean Sea. Rome lay just to the north of the main Grecian colonies of Italy and just south of the Etruscan territories, about 615 miles northwest of Corinth and 1,425 miles northwest of Jerusalem. The hills upon which Rome was built afforded some protection, and its central location in the Mediterranean basin no doubt helped to lead to its prosperity.

In its own mythology, Rome was founded in 753 BCE by twin brothers Romulus and Remus, who were descendants of Aeneas the Trojan of *The Iliad* fame. While the mythological aspects of the story cannot be verified, archaeological exploration has confirmed that the area began to be settled in the eighth century

BCE, and there are likely grains of truth to the historical legend. In all likelihood, the local Latin people began to build a city on some of the hills near the Tiber, and the city began to grow and attract others.

From about 753 to 509, Rome was ruled by kings, some of whom were Etruscan kings from the north. In 509, the native Romans overthrew their Etruscan overlords, and established the Roman Republic (according to legend), ruled by senators with two consuls presiding over them. As time progressed, Rome grew in might and began to dominate the Italian peninsula.

Rome suffered a setback in 386 when Gauls from the north invaded the Italian peninsula and burned the city to the ground. The city was rebuilt and grew stronger than ever. By the third century BCE the Romans began to get entangled with the other western Mediterranean power, the Carthaginians of northern Africa, a former Phoenician colony. In a series of three successive wars in the third and second centuries, Rome defeated Carthage and became the sole power in the western Mediterranean.

Over the next two centuries Rome would extend its dominance to the eastern Mediterranean; by the time of Christ, essentially the entire Mediterranean basin was under the control of Rome. The first century BCE saw major internal dissension within the Roman state, and after a series of generals being dictators over the state, Augustus took command in 44. By about 27 BCE, he had all but become an emperor. Thus the Roman Republic was dissolved, and the Roman Empire was in full force and would remain in some form until the middle of the fifth century CE.

During New Testament times, Rome functioned as both the political and economic capitals of the Empire, and therefore the city was very large and in part transitory. It is estimated that one million people lived there during the time of Christ; likewise, since people were coming and going from every part of the Empire, any new idea or concept would soon find its way to Rome (*cf.* Tacitus, *Annals*, 15.44). Romans, then, were used to hearing all kinds of new ideas and concepts, and it should not surprise us to find the Gospel being preached there from early times.

Rome

Flaminian Gate · Pincian Gate · Nomentian Gate · Vatican Hill · Tomb of Hadrian · Tomb of Augustus · Baths of Diocletian · Praetorian Camp · Circus of Nero · Baths of Nero · Stadium of Domitian · Pantheon · Baths of Constantine · Viminal Hill · Aurelian Wall · Esquiline Hill · Theater of Pompey · Circus Flaminius · Forum · Arch of Titus · Baths of Trajan · Aurelian Gate · Jewish Quarter · Temple of Diana · Palaces · Colosseum · Caelian Hill · Castrensian Amphitheater · Janiculan Hill · Porticus Aemilia · Circus Maximus · Praenestine Way · Aventine Hill · Horrea Galbana · Baths of Caracalla · Latin Gate · Latin Way · Ostian Gate · Ostian Way · Appian Way · Scale of Feet 0—2000 · © 2006 MANNA All Rights Reserved www.biblemaps.com

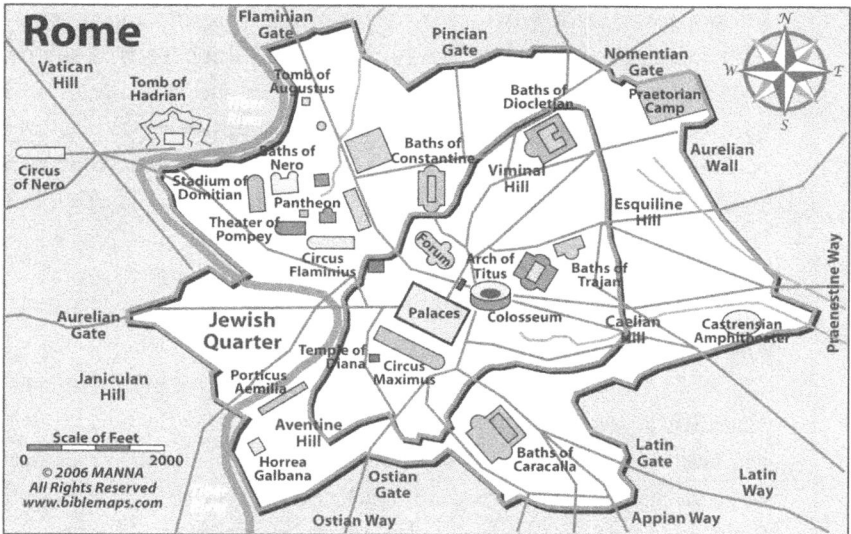

The Founding of the Church in Rome

The beginnings of the church in Rome are shrouded in mystery. We know that there was a church in Rome by 57 CE, when Paul writes to the church there, and that it had been there for some time (Rom 1.8, 11–15). We are told that there are some from Rome present in Jerusalem on the day of Pentecost in 30, likely both Jews and proselytes (Acts 2.10). It is likely that some such persons believed in Jesus on that day and became part of the church (Acts 2.37–38, 41). Others returned to Rome sometime during the 30s.

The only witness that we have of the Gospel being promoted in Rome in those days comes not from the Bible but from a Roman author named Suetonius. In the days of the Roman emperor Claudius (41–54), he wrote:

> Because the Jews at Rome caused continuous disturbances at the instigation of Chrestus, he expelled them from the city. (*The Twelve Caesars*, 5.25)

This is likely the same decree that compelled Aquila and Priscilla to leave Rome and Italy for Corinth (Acts 18.2). It is not known for certain when this decree was given; if Luke intends for us to understand that "lately" in Acts 18.2 means that the decree was recently given and therefore Aquila and Priscilla moved to Corinth not long before Paul arrived, then we would be safe to date the decree sometime between 48–50. It is true that Suetonius calls the person "Chrestus," not "Christ" specifically, but most believe that this is a misunderstanding on the part of the author. As we have already seen, the preaching of the Gospel in the midst of the Jews often led to confrontations, both with Jews and with Gentiles (Acts 8.1; 13.50; 14.2, 5, 19; 16.20–24; 17.5–9, 13; 18.12–18; 19.23–41). It would not be surprising in the least, then, if the Jews of Rome attempted to haul up Christians preaching the Gospel to the rulers in Rome, or if the Gentile Romans themselves put up a fuss about the preaching of the Gospel, and Claudius' reaction was to expel the Jews from the city. We can see, then, that the Gospel was most likely being promoted in Rome by the late 40s, and the authorities even took notice.

Paul Prepares His Way to Rome

The New Testament revelation regarding the church in Rome begins with Paul's intention to visit and to promote the Gospel there. For many years Paul purposed to preach the Gospel where it had not yet been heard at all (Rom 15.20–21; 46–57 CE), but in the Spirit he began to purpose to go to Rome after having gone through Macedonia, Achaia, and Jerusalem (Acts 19.21, 57 CE). To prepare his way to Rome, Paul wrote to the church there, most likely from Corinth, around 57–58 (Rom 16.23; Rom 1.8–13; 15.22–24).

The letter to the Romans is one of Paul's greatest theological treatises, and there is much within the letter that applies to all believers. It would seem, however, that there were some issues going on within the church in Rome that Paul addressed in his letter; it is likely that he would have learned such things from some of his associates that had gone on to Rome before him, including Aquila and Priscilla (Rom 16.3–5).

Perhaps the most fundamental issue within the church was

the relationship between Jewish and Gentile believers in Christ. We do not know how long Claudius' decree was in effect; he died three or four years before the writing of the Roman letter, and Nero was the new emperor. If nothing else, the return of Aquila and Priscilla indicates that if the decree were even still in effect, it was not being enforced; we can safely assume that many of the Jewish Christians returned to Rome, had they even left. Paul spends the first eight chapters of Romans demonstrating first how all have sinned and are in need of redemption (1–3); how Jesus Christ is that redemption for all believers, having fulfilled the Law; how the Law was added later (3–4); that we must all be obedient to Christ; and how, by being obedient, we can have every confidence of our salvation (6–8). In Romans 9–11, Paul establishes how God added the Gentiles into the fold: God certainly had the right to do so, and we have no right to question it (9); all desire that Israel should be saved, but they must hear and repent (10); and the image of the olive tree, with some branches being removed and others grafted in, and the concern that all must have to remain faithful (11).

Paul then turns in Romans 12–16 to handle many specific matters of the faith. All Christians are to be as living and holy sacrifices, not conforming to this world, but being transformed by the renewal of their minds (Rom 12.1–2). Christians must not think of themselves too highly, but realize that they function within a greater whole, described in terms of a body; the church is likened to a human body, with different parts having different roles, all complementing one another, being directed by the Head, Christ (Rom 12.3–6; *cf.* also 1 Cor 12.12–28). Each one, then, is expected to use the gifts he has been given. Christians are to abhor the evil and cling to the good, loving each other and looking out for their interests, along with taking care of their needs (Rom 12.9–10, 13). They are to bless those who persecute them and to be at peace with all men as much as it depends on them (Rom 12.14, 18). In all things, good should conquer evil (Rom 12.9–21). Paul goes on to establish that Christians are to respect and obey governments and pay their taxes and to love their neighbors as themselves (Rom 13).

Romans 14–15.1 provides a description of a circumstance causing problems in Rome. Some brethren, labeled the "strong," believe that they have the right to eat all foods; other brethren, labeled as the "weak" do not believe that they can eat meat (Rom 14.2). Some believe that the matter under consideration is meat sacrificed to idols; while that is a possibility, the full context of the Roman letter favors the interpretation that the matter at hand are Jewish cleanliness laws (*cf.* "observing of days," Rom 14.5; Col 2.14–17). Regardless, Paul indicates throughout Romans 14 many important considerations: both groups are not to set each other at naught (v 3); Christians should resolve not to put a stumbling-block in another's way (v 13); there is liberty in matters of "food and drink" but not in "righteousness, peace, and joy in the Holy Spirit" (v 17); it is not good to do anything by which your brother stumbles (v 21); Christians should watch lest they be condemned in what they approve (v 22); and Christians should act only by faith, for what is not of faith is sin (v 23). Likewise, Paul indicates the responsibility of brethren who are stronger to bear with and build up the weak brethren, seeking the best for each other, as Christ did for all (Rom 15.1–3). In the end, we are to receive one another, just as Christ received us (Rom 15.4–7).

Paul was convinced that the Roman brethren were strong enough to admonish one another and that they were filled with goodness and knowledge (Rom 15.14), but he desired to provide some spiritual benefit for them so that they may be established, finding comfort in each other's faith (Rom 1.11). He hoped to go and find rest with the brethren in Rome (Rom 15.32).

Paul also felt compelled to warn the Romans to mark those who taught doctrines contrary to the truth, and to turn from them (Rom 16.16–17). Paul did so not because they were disobedient, but to make sure that they remained steadfast and were not deceived (Rom 16.18–19).

We can see, therefore, that the church in Rome in 57 was relatively strong, obedient to the Lord and full of goodness and knowledge, but had some difficulties on account of Jewish and Gentile distinctions. Paul's warm reception from the brethren in

Rome three years later indicates that the letter was well-received (Acts 28.15), and we should have no doubt that the Romans followed Paul's advice.

Paul and Rome, 58–67
After Paul wrote the letter to the Romans, he traveled back through Macedonia, sailed around Asia Minor, and arrived in Caesarea (Acts 20.2–21.8). Paul then visited the brethren in Jerusalem and was encouraged to go to the Temple to honor the customs of the Jews (Acts 21.9–26). While there, some Jews from Asia supposed that he had brought a Gentile into the Temple with him and began an uproar that led to Paul's imprisonment (Acts 21.27–40). After being transferred to Caesarea, Paul remained in prison during the time of Felix's rule over Judea until the beginning of Festus' rule (Acts 23.18–24.27; 58–59 CE). When Paul was brought before Festus, Paul appealed to Caesar, and his appeal was granted (Acts 25.1–12; 60 CE). After a long and difficult journey, Paul arrived in Italy (Acts 27.1–28.12). After going from Syracuse to Rhegium to Puteoli, finding brethren in the last place (Acts 28.12–14), Paul made it to Rome, having been accompanied by brethren from Rome from the Three Taverns (Acts 28.15).

Paul was left under house arrest, with people able to come to him (Acts 28.16, 30; 60–62 CE). He first called the highly respected Jews of the city to him and preached Jesus to them (Acts 18.17–28). Some believed, and some disputed (as happened almost everywhere), and Paul turned to preach to the Gentiles. Luke ends the book of Acts by establishing that Paul was under house arrest for two years in Rome, preaching the Gospel without hindrance (Acts 28.30–31).

It was during this imprisonment that Paul wrote the letters to Ephesus, Philippi, and Colossae. We learn from Philippians 4.22 that there are some members of Caesar's own household who are saints and who especially desire to greet the Philippian brethren.

What happens after the imprisonment is not precisely known, since the book of Acts ends with this imprisonment. Based upon the evidence previously established in Acts regarding the Romans' view of Paul (Acts 25.18–21; 26.32), Paul was most likely cleared of any charge of wrongdoing on this occasion and was set free. Since Paul's presence in Macedonia and Crete cannot be otherwise reconciled in the Acts narrative, it is likely that he then visited at least these places after his imprisonment (1 Tim 1.3; Tit 1.5), and may have finally made it to Spain (Rom 15.24).

On the other hand, it is clear that by 2 Timothy Paul is back in prison, and the situation looks grim (2 Tim 1.12; 4.16–18). It is most likely that he is back in prison in Rome, and died in prison or by execution soon after writing the letter. Later tradition established that Paul was beheaded in Rome by the order of the Emperor Nero (Eusebius, *History of the Church* 2.25.5).

Paul's martyrdom most likely had something to do with the persecutions of Christians in Rome that occurred sometime between 64–68. In 64, Rome suffered a great fire. The cause of the blaze is often disputed, but two results were not: Nero took the opportunity to make Rome a more aesthetically pleasing city (including making a golden house for himself), and he blamed the fire on Christians (*cf.* Tacitus, *Annals* 15.44). Christians were then subjected to wild beasts or nailed to crosses and burned alive *(ibid.)*. We do not know if this persecution spread beyond Rome, but we do see that Christians were at that point seen as distinct from Jews (which was likely not the case even ten years previously) and that the brethren in Rome suffered greatly at the hands of Nero. Based upon the likelihood of Paul traveling between his imprisonments, it is more likely that he died later in this period rather than earlier (*ca.* 65–67). In the end, Rome represented the end of Paul's earthly work for Christ.

Peter and Rome

Paul is not the only apostle attested by tradition as dying in Rome at the time; the same traditions establish that Peter was crucified in Rome (Eusebius, *History of the Church* 2.25.5). In the New Testament, Peter's role after the Jerusalem council is shrouded in some obscurity. In our study we have seen that Peter was in Antioch when Paul opposed him (Gal 2.1–14), and such potentially occurred in about 53–54. Likewise, Peter is known in Corinth (1 Cor 1.12; 3.22), and it is likely then that he at least visited there between 52 and 57.

From there it would seem that Peter traveled to Rome. According to 1 Peter 5.13, Peter wrote 1 Peter from "Babylon." While some believe that he speaks of actual Babylon in modern-day Iraq, we have no evidence from any source that would substantiate such a view. It is most likely that Peter wrote from Rome, which he calls "Babylon" in code. That Rome is referred to as Babylon is indicated in Revelation (*cf.* Rev 18); likewise, Peter indicates that Mark "his son" is with him, identified usually as the same John Mark whom Paul desired Timothy to bring with him to Rome (2 Tim 4.11). Most likely, therefore, Peter wrote to the brethren of Asia Minor from Rome (*cf.* 1 Pet 1.1; 5.13).

Peter indicates in his letter that he is an elder and encourages his fellow elders (1 Pet 5.1–4); this does not make him the only elder in Rome, but it does indicate the presence of an eldership and Peter's role within it.

We do not know much about Peter's role in Rome, but it seems fairly clear that he spent some time there as an elder and met his end there also. Such by no means, however, justifies the current beliefs of the Roman Catholic Church in terms of Rome being the "chair of Peter" or any such thing.

Rome After the Apostles, 70–115
Such ends the New Testament revelation regarding the church in Rome; however, there were some writers living in Rome and writing to Rome right after the period of the apostles that help to shed some light on the church as it continued.

The letter of *1 Clement* is a letter from the church in Rome to the church in Corinth, likely written around 70. The author speaks of "successive and calamitous events" that occurred among them, which may refer to some of the persecutions suffered under Nero (*1 Clement* 1). Likewise, it would seem that the church in Corinth requested some kind of advice from the church in Rome *(ibid)*. This is not spoken of in terms of authority; the author is careful to keep the entire letter as a collective exhortation, and we get no impression that the church in Rome is imposing its will on the church in Corinth. The letter indicates that the church in Rome, despite suffering persecution, remains respected for its stand for the truth.

Around 115, Ignatius of Antioch wrote a letter to Rome as he was heading there for his martyrdom. He did not want the Roman Christians to hinder him from his martyrdom (Ignatius, *Letter to the Romans*, 2). Surprisingly, Ignatius issues no command to Rome to respect the bishop as he did to other churches; this indicates that either Rome would not hear Ignatius about these things, that Rome already had that system and had no problem with it, or that Ignatius was more concerned about his martyrdom than anything else going on in Rome. He does ask them to pray for the "church in Syria" that is losing its "shepherd" in himself (9), and so unfortunately the middle or latter options are most likely.

Being in the capital city of the Empire, the church in Rome would be constantly challenged by the false teachings of Marcion, other Gnostics, and other false teachers in the second century, while they themselves were clearly caught up in the "bishop over elders" system of hierarchy that has no New Testament precedent. We all know where this system in Rome eventually led; nevertheless, much can be learned from the church in Rome while it remained faithful.

Conclusion

Since Rome was a "happening" place, the church in Rome had much going on within it. Its origins are shrouded in some mystery, but by the time of the 50s and 60s, a relatively strong church has developed, full of knowledge and goodness, having some Jewish-Gentile differences as the main doctrinal problem. The church in Rome suffered greatly under persecution, with both Paul and Peter dying there for the cause of Christ. The church remained respected and firm for some time, but even they got caught up in the second century apostasy and would later become the center of the apostasy in terms of the Roman Catholic Church. Nevertheless, the church in Rome in the New Testament stands as a witness that a church can grow and develop without having an apostle present and without being founded by an apostle. The Gospel can be spread right in the heart of a power contrary to the Lord Jesus, and the church in Rome reminds us that God is over all. Let us take heart and be strengthened, just as the church in Rome was.

Colossae

If then ye were raised together with Christ, seek the things that are above, where Christ is, seated on the right hand of God. (Col 3.1)

The church in Colossae represented a unique situation: a younger church without the benefit of apostolic foundation where different doctrines were being advocated. Despite his imprisonment and relative unfamiliarity with the brethren there, Paul wrote a letter to the Colossian Christians to try to build them up in their faith and to direct them properly in Christ.

Geography and History

Colossae was part of the Roman province of Asia, part of ancient Phrygia, in modern Turkey. The city was a bit more than 100 miles inland from Ephesus on the Halys River and was situated on the highway from Ephesus into Mesopotamia; Laodicea was twelve miles away. Colossae was 108 miles southwest of Antioch of Pisidia and 530 miles northwest of Jerusalem.

A significant way station on the main road through Asia Minor during the Hellenistic period, Colossae began to fade as Laodicea and Hierapolis gained prominence during the Roman period. Colossae suffered greatly from the earthquake that decimated the region in around 60 or 61 CE; the city never really recovered, and the city of Chonae was built near its ruins. This may explain why the church is present when Paul writes to them in the early 60s but is not mentioned by John as one of the churches of Asia in the 90s.

The whole area was known for wool production and for its presence on the main highway through Asia Minor. Colossae attracted a mixture of native Phrygians, Jews, Greeks, and Romans, and the church reflected this type of mixture. The Gospel found fertile ground in Colossae, as we shall see.

The Origins of the Church in Colossae

The church in Colossae, like the church in Rome, began without having been founded by an apostle. Its origins, also like Rome's, are somewhat mysterious. There were Jews from Asia present in Jerusalem on the day of Pentecost in 30 (Acts 2.9); it might have been that some Colossian Jews were present—and perhaps some may have believed—but such is entirely conjectural.

The origins of the church in Colossae best correlate to the time of Paul in Ephesus, between 55–57 CE. We are told in Acts 19.10 that on account of the work of Paul in Ephesus, the word of God was preached to "all Asia," both "Jews and Greeks." Colossae is in Asia, and it is possible that the Colossians heard the Gospel from Paul in Ephesus. Nevertheless, he does not betray familiarity with many of them in his letter. In his letter, Paul mentions the work of Epaphras among the Colossians, describing him as a "fellow servant" of Paul, a "faithful minister" on his behalf (Col 1.7; 4.12). It is perhaps best to conclude that Epaphras the Colossian—and maybe some others (Onesimus? Philemon?)—heard the Gospel from Paul, converted, and then began promoting the Gospel in Colossae. Epaphras also promoted the Gospel in Laodicea and Hierapolis (Col 4.13), and it is likely that others went into the other cities in Asia; thus Luke is able to say that "all Asia" heard the word of the Lord, both from Paul and from these native sons who converted.

Regardless, the church in Colossae saw its greatest growth roughly between 55 and 60, precipitated by the work of Epaphras among them.

Paul and Difficulties in Colossae

Although the church was growing, not all was well. During Paul's imprisonment, either in Caesarea or Rome (58–62), Epaphras

visited Paul for some unspecified reason (Col 4.12). Epaphras no doubt provided a report of the goings-on in Colossae and Laodicea, and Paul was prompted to write letters to these churches (Col 4.16). (While some believe that the Ephesian letter was really to Laodicea, there is no proof of this; for all intents and purposes the Laodicean letter has been lost.) Paul sent these letters (with the letter to the Ephesians and probably also Philemon) to them via Tychicus (Col 4.7).

Paul encourages the brethren in Colossae to continue to grow in the knowledge of Christ, walking worthily of Him (Col 1.9–11). His primary concern, however, was that the Colossians should continue in the faith, grounded and steadfast within it (Col 1.23; 2.6–7).

Some of the specific problems are made manifest in Colossians 2, and they seem to include both Jewish and Hellenistic/proto-Gnostic matters. Paul begins with the Hellenistic matters, first emphasizing that Christ is the source of wisdom and knowledge (Col 2.2–3). Paul says this so that the brethren in Colossae are not deluded by persuasive speech to the contrary (Col 2.4). The main difficulty is made manifest in Colossians 2.8–9:

> Take heed lest there shall be any one that maketh spoil of you
> through his philosophy and vain deceit, after the tradition of
> men, after the rudiments of the world, and not after Christ: for
> in him dwelleth all the fulness of the Godhead bodily.

"Philosophy" and "vain deceit" are most parallel to Greek
forms of philosophy, most of which were based in attempts to
understand the nature of the physical world and the attempt to
extrapolate human conduct on its basis. Since Paul finds it necessary to emphasize the humanity of Jesus in verse 9, it very well
may be that some of the brethren in Colossae or those who were
influencing the brethren were attempting to promote a docetic
view of Jesus—that is, that He only seemed to be flesh, but was
not truly flesh. This view was more acceptable to Greeks, especially those enmeshed in philosophy; to such persons, God in the
flesh was an abominable concept. Such a view has many affinities
with the later Gnostic heresy, and it may well be that the views
promoted in Colossae represent a form of proto-Gnosticism. Regardless, the brethren in Colossae were not to focus on philosophy
or the natural world as much as the truth of God in Christ Jesus,
through whom all was created (Col 1.15–17).

Paul then turns to the Jewish matters of difficulty. He emphasizes that the Colossians were circumcised not by hands but in
Christ, having been buried with Him in baptism (Col 2.11–12).
Paul then establishes that when the Colossians were still in their
sins and separated from God, God made them alive with Him
by taking the bond of ordinances out of the way, having nailed it
to the cross (Col 2.13–15; *cf.* Eph 2.11–18). While the statement
made in Colossians 2.14 would seem vague—after all, what is this
bond of ordinances?—the conclusion makes things clear:

> Let no man therefore judge you in meat, or in drink, or in respect
> of a feast day or a new moon or a sabbath day: which are a shadow
> of the things to come; but the body is Christ's. (Col 2.16–17)

Romans 14 indicates how important these matters are to the
Jewish Christians of the day, and Paul wants it made clear to the

Colossians that they are matters of liberty, since they are but a shadow of the reality in Christ. Therefore, we see that there are also Jewish Christians in Colossae (or perhaps Jews or Jewish Christians somehow influencing the Christians in Colossae) desiring to bind matters of Jewish conscience on the brethren.

Paul then continues to warn the brethren against following after people who are puffed up based on visions that they have supposedly seen, attempting to steer the brethren away from the true faith in Christ (Col 2.18–19). Paul concludes the second chapter as follows:

> If ye died with Christ from the rudiments of the world, why, as though living in the world, do ye subject yourselves to ordinances, "Handle not, nor taste, nor touch" (all which things are to perish with the using), after the precepts and doctrines of men? Which things have indeed a show of wisdom in will-worship, and humility, and severity to the body; but are not of any value against the indulgence of the flesh. (Col 2.20–23)

Such ascetic concepts—the belief that avoidance of certain physical things can lead to greater godliness and holiness—would work either in Hellenistic proto-Gnosticism or in Judaism. Paul warns against this strictly, demonstrating that avoiding foods or other such things does not actually help one to avoid the temptations of the flesh.

The church in Colossae was thus beset with many difficulties from different quarters: some brethren promoted Hellenistic philosophical concepts, willing to compromise with certain important tenets of Christianity to make it conform to Hellenistic thought, while other brethren wished to promote Jewish observances and dietary restrictions. Some of these, all of them, or perhaps another group also strove to seem great among the church on account of visions they had received that were not in concord with the will of Christ, striving to persuade the brethren to engage in asceticism in an attempt to demonstrate "holiness." We can easily understand how Epaphras would be overwhelmed and how the situation would require one with greater authority to correct the brethren!

Nothing more is said about the brethren in Colossae, but we hope that they corrected themselves and were found firm and steadfast in Christ.

Apostolic Instruction to Colossae

Paul also took the opportunity afforded him in writing to the Colossians to establish many important instructions to the brethren in regard to the faith. Most of these instructions involve individual conduct, and many have parallels with instruction given in Ephesians.

Colossians 3.1–4 presents the main theme of Paul's instruction: the brethren are to set their minds on the things above, the things of God, and not on earthly matters, since they had died to them and should now live for God. On account of this, Paul encourages them to avoid immorality caused by earthly passions (Col 3.5–11). They are also to manifest the fruit of the Spirit toward one another, being loving, compassionate, kind, patient, and longsuffering toward one another (Col 3.12–14). Paul also establishes that the peace and word of Christ should dwell within them, and that they should teach and admonish one another in song (Col 3.15–16). All things should be done in the name of Christ, and prayer should be offered to the Father through Him (Col 3.17).

Paul then goes on to provide instruction to people in different stations, similar to his instruction in Ephesians 5.23–6.9. Wives are to be subject to their husbands, husbands are to love their wives, children should obey their parents, fathers should not provoke their children, servants should obey their masters and work as to the Lord, and masters are to remember that they have a Master in Heaven (Col 3.18–4.1).

Paul charges the Colossians to walk wisely among those who are not Christians, redeeming the time, and to speak as seasoned with salt, knowing how to properly answer each person (Col 4.5–6).

Since so many of these instructions find parallels in other letters, we should not presuppose that these were actual problems any more in Colossae than in Ephesus, Laodicea, or in other places. Paul provides exhortations regarding many matters of the faith to remind brethren to "walk worthily of Christ."

Philemon and Onesimus

It is profitable to consider Paul's short letter to Philemon in the context of the church in Colossae, since Onesimus, the slave of Philemon (Phlm 10), is explicitly identified as a Colossian (Col 4.9), and Archippus, a member of Philemon's household and an addressee of the letter (Phlm 2), is addressed as a member of the church in Colossae (Col 4.17). Most likely, Philemon was a member of the church in Colossae, and it would seem that the church there met in his house (Phlm 2).

Although not all the details of the situation are provided, we know that Onesimus, who was a slave of Philemon, ended up being either in Caesarea or Rome with Paul (Col 4.9), and Paul was sending him back to Colossae. It is most likely, then, that Paul sent Colossians and Philemon at the same time, around 58 to 60. Paul was concerned for the welfare of Onesimus, for Onesimus had wronged Philemon, likely leaving with Epaphras or someone else without Philemon's consent (Phlm 15–18). Philemon 10 gives the impression that Onesimus was not a Christian before meeting Paul, but he was being sent back to Colossae as a brother in Christ. Paul, therefore, desired that Philemon be accepted back as a brother and not beaten or otherwise harmed for his conduct (Phlm 19–20).

Paul knew that as an apostle of Christ he had the ability to speak strongly to Philemon, commanding him to do what he ought (Phlm 8); instead, he appealed to Philemon gently and lovingly, willing to be charged for the wrong incurred by Onesimus (Phlm 9, 18–19). Nevertheless, Paul fully expected Philemon to treat Onesimus well, perhaps rejoicing that he had not just received back his servant, but had also gained a brother in Christ (Phlm 16, 20–21). Paul also hoped that Philemon would prepare him a place to stay, for he hoped to visit him after his imprisonment (Phlm 20).

It is clear from the letter to Philemon that God does not automatically condemn the practice of owning slaves, but that God does expect masters to treat their slaves, especially slaves that are fellow Christians, well. We can learn from such encounters that even though Christians may have different social standing, we should all still love one another and treat one another as equals, not making distinction (*cf.* Jas 2.1–7). If Philemon could accept Onesimus, we can all accept one another!

Conclusion

It is unfortunate that Colossae ends in tragedy. The earthquake in 60 or 61 spelled doom for the city: since Paul betrays no knowledge of the disaster, it is most likely that the letters of Colossians and Philemon were written before the event or before knowledge of the event spread. We do not know how long Colossae remained after the earthquake, but most of the brethren probably would have dispersed to Hierapolis, Laodicea, or other Asian cities after the event, with some perhaps being part of Chonae that was built afterward. Regardless, Colossae is not considered one of the churches of Asia in Revelation, and nothing more is mentioned of the city or the church there.

Nevertheless, we can gain much from the example of this short-lived church. We can understand the difficulty presented when people from different worldviews convert and become part of a local church and yet wish to keep said worldviews. The Colossians needed to learn to stop being Jews and Greeks and start being Christians, looking to Christ and no one else. We can see that churches can begin and grow without being founded by an apostle, and yet we learn how important it is for churches to follow apostolic teaching and to focus on the Head, Christ. Let us follow Paul's advice to the Colossians, leaving behind the things of this world and looking to that which is above.

Smyrna, Pergamum, and Thyatira

I was in the Spirit on the Lord's day, and I heard behind me a great voice, as of a trumpet saying, "What thou seest, write in a book and send it to the seven churches: unto Ephesus, and unto Smyrna, and unto Pergamum, and unto Thyatira, and unto Sardis, and unto Philadelphia, and unto Laodicea." (Rev 1.10–11)

We have now examined the majority of New Testament churches; while we could perhaps speak some of the churches in Crete based on Paul's letter to Titus and we know of other churches mentioned quickly in other contexts (churches in Judea and Samaria, Acts 8; Cyprus, Acts 13; *etc.)*, not much is revealed about these churches, and the instruction provided in Titus has also been seen elsewhere.

We are left, then, with six of the seven churches in Asia concerning which John the apostle received revelation while on the island of Patmos, most likely in the latter years of the time of Domitian the emperor of Rome (81–96 CE; see "Ephesus," 67–79, for more on dating the book of Revelation). Let us then consider what Jesus says to the churches in Smyrna, Pergamum, and Thyatira.

Geography and History

Smyrna (modern Izmir), Pergamum (modern Bergama), and Thyatira (modern Akhisar) are all part of the ancient Roman province of Asia in modern day Turkey. These three churches represent a "northern triangle" of the seven churches of Asia Minor, with Ephesus to the southwest and Sardis, Philadelphia, and Laodicea on roughly a straight line to the southeast. Smyrna

is about 47 miles south of Pergamum and southwest of Thyatira;
Pergamum is about 37 miles northwest of Thyatira. Smyrna is
about 36 miles north of Ephesus, while Pergamum is 81 miles
north and Thyatira 71 miles northwest of Ephesus. All three
cities are about 650–680 miles northwest of Jerusalem.

Smyrna, like Ephesus, was a city on the Aegean Sea, located
on a gulf that provided an excellent port, making the city a major
trading center. One could travel inland from Smyrna on a road
following the Hermus River valley to Sardis and Philadelphia
further inland. Pergamum and Thyatira were both located further
north, along the Caicus River; Pergamum was about 15 miles
inland, and Thyatira was even further inland. Pergamum was
known for its library and was the first place where parchment
(animal skin used as a writing surface) was used. Pergamum was
best known, however, for its many pagan temples, especially
the Temple to Zeus; it may be that this temple and its altar is
what Jesus has in mind when He says that Satan's throne is in
Pergamum (Rev 2.13). Thyatira was known especially for its trade
guilds and its dye-manufacturing facilities; after all, Lydia the
seller of purple was from Thyatira (Acts 16.14).

While all three cities had roots in history before the Greeks,
they rise to prominence as Greek colonies or under Greek influence.
Smyrna especially was important to the Greeks as a major port in
Asia Minor; Greek colonists likely established themselves there
by 1000 BCE. All three cities fell to the power of Lydia around
the seventh century; by 530, however, they all were under Persian
authority. Despite constant revolt and some moments of relative
independence, all three cities remained under Persian control
until the time of Alexander the Great in 332.

Alexander's general Lysimachus was given control over the
area after the death of the former, but his "Kingdom of Thrace"
did not last long. Real power shifted to Pergamum and the line
of Attalid kings that ruled there from 238–133. The kings of
Pergamum, then, ruled over all the cities under discussion during
this period, being loyal supporters of Rome and enemies of the
Macedonian Seleucids to the south. When Attalus III died in 133

BCE without an heir, he bequeathed his kingdom to the Romans, and the Romans then ruled it throughout the period of the New Testament as the province of Asia.

The Founding of Churches in Asia

The New Testament does not record any specific information as to the founding of the churches in Smyrna, Pergamum, or Thyatira. Some have hypothesized that Lydia returned to Thyatira and was active in the founding of the church there (*cf.* Acts 16.14, *ca.* 50–51 CE); while this is possible, we have no substantive evidence for the claim. Whatever can be known about the founding of these three churches will be found in the story of the establishment of the church in the province of Asia.

We have previously seen that Asia was a fertile field for the Gospel. It is revealed that some Jews from Asia were in Jerusalem on the day of Pentecost in 30 CE and heard the Gospel from Peter and the apostles (Acts 2.10); while it is likely that some such Jews were part of the 3,000 who were baptized that day (Acts 2.38–41), we have no clear information as to which cities they came from or any preaching they would have done when they returned to Asia.

The church in Asia begins in earnest around 55–57 with Paul's stay in Ephesus (Acts 19.8–10). It is revealed that "all Asia," both Jews and Greeks, heard the Word of God during this time (Acts 19.10), and as we saw with Colossae, this was probably achieved by native sons hearing the Gospel from Paul, converting, and then taking the message themselves to their home cities. While it is possible that Paul might have traveled to cities like Smyrna, Pergamum, or Thyatira during his stay in Ephesus, it is more plausible to believe that people from these cities heard the Gospel from Paul, believed it and converted, and then set to work promoting the Gospel in their native towns.

Regardless, it is evident that by the 90s, there were churches throughout the province of Asia, including churches established in Smyrna, Pergamum, and Thyatira.

Smyrna: Poverty, Riches, and Tribulation

All that is revealed about Smyrna in the New Testament may be found in Revelation 2.8–11:

> And to the angel of the church in Smyrna write: "These things saith the first and the last, who was dead, and lived again: I know thy tribulation, and thy poverty (but thou art rich), and the blasphemy of them that say they are Jews, and they art not, but are a synagogue of Satan. Fear not the things which thou art about to suffer: behold, the devil is about to cast some of you into prison, that ye may be tried; and ye shall have tribulation ten days. Be thou faithful unto death, and I will give thee the crown of life. He that hath an ear, let him hear what the Spirit saith to the churches. He that overcometh shall not be hurt of the second death."

We can gain some information about the church in Smyrna from this text. The church seemed to have been made up mostly of people who were poor according to worldly standards, yet were truly rich in Christ (Rev 2.9; *cf.* 2 Cor 8.9). They were currently suffering great tribulation, especially from Jews: while the Jews professed belief in the One True God, they certainly did not live according to His will by persecuting the Christians in Smyrna (Rev 2.9).

Jesus spoke of the church in Smyrna in favorable terms, not having anything negative to say about them. He does warn them about upcoming difficulties and how some will even be imprisoned for the Name (Rev 2.10). Jesus enjoined obedience upon them, confirming that if they are faithful to death, they will be granted eternal life (Rev 2.10).

We also have some additional information regarding Smyrna in later literature. Polycarp—who wrote a letter to the Philippians, was believed to be an associate of John, and the teacher of Irenaeus—is "bishop" of Smyrna; whether he believed himself to be one of many elders or a sole bishop is not known. Ignatius of Antioch wrote a letter to the church in Smyrna around 115, warning the brethren to avoid the Gnostic heresies (Ignatius, *Letter to the Smyrneans* 4–5), repeating his desire for them to follow the

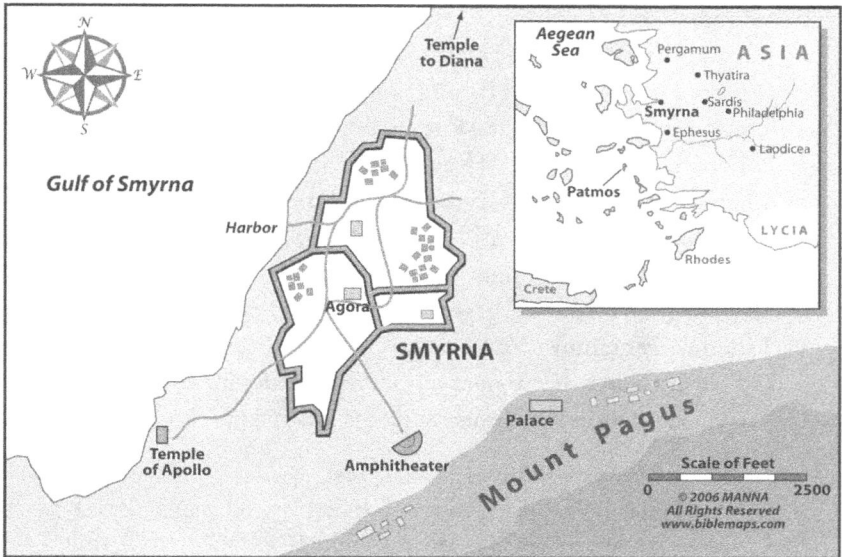

"bishop" and the elders (even establishing that the Lord's Supper can only be administered by a bishop or his deputy), and declaring that baptism must be seen by the bishop (*ibid.*, 8). It is possible that this was written because the brethren in Smyrna rejected the idea of one elder having more authority than others, but it is more likely that Ignatius was enjoining upon them practices that they had seen in other churches and were likely doing themselves. It is unfortunate that the church in Smyrna would so soon drift into such error after John wrote to them.

The church in Smyrna was stable. Jesus spoke well of it. Its members may not have had the most in terms of physical wealth, but they were rich toward God; they were currently suffering tribulation and persecution and would suffer some more, but to them was extended the promise of eternal life for their faithfulness. While the later end of the church in Smyrna is lamentable, we can gain encouragement from their example as they stood at the end of the first century.

Pergamum: Following After Balaam

Jesus, speaking of Himself as "He that hath the sharp two-edged sword" (Rev 2.12), then turned to address the church in Pergamum (Rev 2.12–17).

Jesus began by establishing some positive things regarding the church in Pergamum. He knew that they dwell in a difficult place, "where Satan's throne is" (Rev 2.13). This is likely a reference to the altar in the Temple of Zeus and indicates that the Christians in Pergamum lived in the midst of a very idolatrous and hostile people. The brethren in Pergamum had not denied the faith in Christ Jesus despite great trial and persecution; one of them, Antipas, was even killed in Pergamum for his faith (Rev 2.13).

Nevertheless, there were serious difficulties in Pergamum which required attention, as Jesus indicates in Revelation 2.14–15:

> But I have a few things against thee, because thou hast there some that hold the teaching of Balaam, who taught Balak to cast a stumbling block before the children of Israel, to eat things sacrificed to idols, and to commit fornication. So hast thou also some that hold the teaching of the Nicolaitans in like manner.

It would seem that Jesus is comparing some of the brethren in Pergamum—those who hold to the teaching of the Nicolaitans—to Balaam of the Old Testament. In Numbers 22.1–6, Balak the king of Moab summoned Balaam to come and curse the people of Israel who encamped near him. Balaam was a man who believed in God, and God forbade him to curse Israel (Num 22.7–13). Balaam eventually went and provided blessings upon Israel rather than curses (Num 23–24). Even though Balaam outwardly acted as an agent of God, he then turned and undermined God's people by counseling Balak to have the women of Moab seduce the men of Israel and also to worship other gods, which Balak then did successfully (Num 25.1–3; 31.8–16).

Therefore, just as Balaam indirectly overthrew the people of God, so these who adhere to the doctrine of the Nicolaitans (sharing of wives among brethren based upon the supposed teaching of Nicolaus; see "Ephesus," 67–79, for more) were undermining the brethren in Pergamum. It may be that the Nicolaitans were also persuading the people to worship other gods and sacrifice

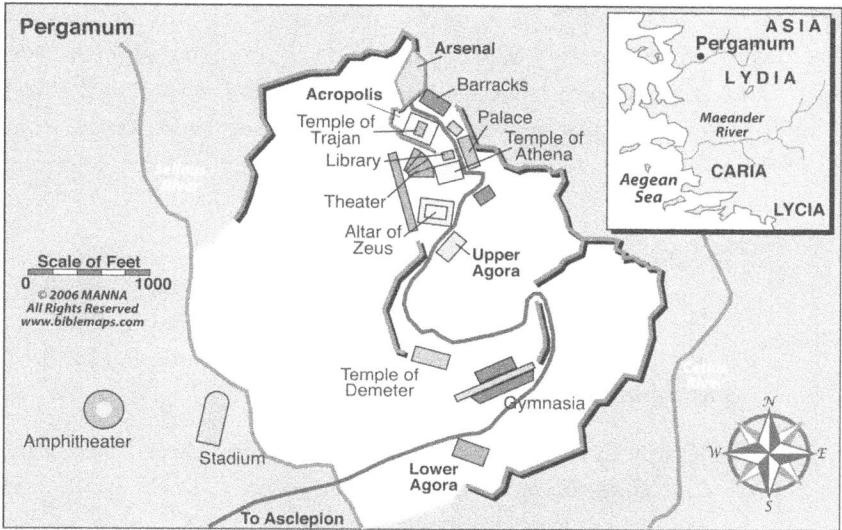

to them; it is more plausible, however, that Jesus is making a parallel between the "teaching of Balaam" and the "teaching of the Nicolaitans," and so it is the teachings involved and not the practices that are commensurate. Regardless, as Paul established, "a little leaven leavens the whole lump" (1 Cor 5.6; Gal 5.9), and that was what was occurring in Pergamum.

Jesus is not ambiguous about what should happen: repentance, or else Jesus would come and make war against them "by the sword of [His] mouth" (Rev 2.16). This would not be a pleasant fate!

We can thus see the condition of the church in Pergamum in the 90s. While many stood firm in the face of persecution, some of the brethren adhered to the doctrine of the Nicolaitans by participating in sexual immorality and threatened to seduce all the brethren into their belief system. Jesus strictly charged them to repent or to face His wrath; we can only hope that they heeded His warning!

Thyatira: The Faithful and Jezebel

Jesus spoke next to the church in Thyatira (Rev 2.18–28). His instruction to the brethren may be considered in two parts: Jesus' words to the faithful and His words to "Jezebel" and her followers.

In Revelation 2.19, Jesus commended the faithful brethren for their conduct: they have proper love, faith, ministry, and patience, and as opposed to Ephesus, their works are more than at the first (*cf.* Rev 2.4–5). Jesus told these Christians to hold fast to what they have until He comes (Rev 2.25), and provided the following encouragement in Revelation 2.26–28:

> And he that overcometh, and he that keepeth my works unto the end, to him will I give authority over the nations: and he shall rule them with a rod of iron, as the vessels of the potter are broken to shivers; as I also have received of my Father: and I will give him the morning star.

The only thing that Jesus had against the brethren in Thyatira was that they tolerated the "woman Jezebel" (Rev 2.20). She professed herself as a prophetess and seduced Christians to commit sexually deviant behavior and to eat food sacrificed to idols (Rev 2.20). Such people have "know[n] the deep things of Satan" (Rev 2.24). Whether she had connections with the Nicolaitans is not revealed; likewise, no connection is made between her and the situation in Pergamum. "Jezebel" is not likely to be the real name of the person involved; Jesus is most likely making reference to the infamous wife of Ahab, daughter of Ethbaal king of Sidon, who compelled Israel to worship Baal (1 Kings 16.31).

The fate of "Jezebel" was sealed: she would be cast upon the bed of tribulation since she has not repented of her works (Rev 2.21–22). Those who follow after her will suffer the same fate if they do not repent themselves; otherwise, they will die, and Jesus will be magnified and praised because of it (Rev 2.22–23).

It is manifest that the church in Thyatira had been invaded by a false prophet of some form—a woman if the imagery is consistent with reality—and this false prophet has seduced many Christians in Thyatira to commit iniquity. The rest of the brethren were called upon not to "tolerate" or "suffer" this person, but we do not see any specific directive for the church to take any action against them. The rest were merely to "hold fast," and have nothing to do with these teachings (Rev 2.24–25). Perhaps they would simply avoid these errant brethren; perhaps Jesus would take care of the problem for them.

The church in Thyatira in the 90s had two main parties: the group that was faithful to God, to whom Jesus requires no additional burden than to remain firm and not tolerate the errant ones in their midst; and the group following "Jezebel" and being led into destruction and ruin. We can only hope that most of the brethren following "Jezebel" repented and returned to the faith.

Conclusion

Although Jesus wrote by the hand of John to three different churches, Smyrna, Pergamum, and Thyatira, the messages presented were consistent. The brethren in Smyrna and Pergamum faced persecution from those who are without. The brethren in Pergamum and Thyatira faced immoral brethren from within. Jesus encouraged them all to remain faithful to Him and called the errant to repentance. Churches throughout time have suffered from similar situations—difficulties from without and within— and we would do well to gain wisdom from what Jesus says to the churches in Asia. Indeed, "he that hath an ear, let him hear what the Spirit says to the churches" (Rev 2.7, 11, 17, 29).

Sardis, Philadelphia, and Laodicea

I was in the Spirit on the Lord's day, and I heard behind me a great
voice, as of a trumpet saying, "What thou seest, write in a book and
send it to the seven churches: unto Ephesus, and unto Smyrna, and
unto Pergamum, and unto Thyatira, and unto Sardis, and unto
Philadelphia, and unto Laodicea." (Rev 1.10–11)

As we are concluding our analysis of the churches of the New Testament proper, six of the seven churches in Asia remained. These
are the churches concerning which John the Apostle received revelation while on the island of Patmos, most likely in the latter
years of the time of Domitian the emperor of Rome (81–96 CE;
see "Ephesus," 67–79, for more on dating Revelation). We have
investigated the churches in Smyrna, Pergamum, and Thyatira;
let us conclude with what Jesus says to the churches in Sardis,
Philadephia, and Laodicea.

Geography and History

Sardis, Philadelphia (modern Alasehir), and Laodicea are all
part of the ancient Roman province of Asia in modern day Turkey. These three churches represent a southeast line of the seven
churches of Asia Minor, with Ephesus to the west and Smyrna,
Pergamum, and Thyatira all to the north and northwest. Sardis
is about 25 miles northwest of Philadelphia and 70 miles northwest of Laodicea; Philadelphia is about 48 miles northwest of
Laodicea. Sardis is about 56 miles northeast of Ephesus, while
Philadelphia is 70 miles northeast of Ephesus and Laodicea is 97

miles east of Ephesus. All three cities are about 550–615 miles northwest of Jerusalem.

Both Sardis and Philadelphia were located near Mount Tmolus in inland Asia. Sardis' position was especially beneficial, being almost impregnable along the northern slope of the mountain and standing at the junction of the main roads heading to the sea. Sardis was especially known for its woolen garment manufacturing. Philadelphia lay within the main wine production area of Asia Minor and was a wealthy trade center. Dionysus, the Greek god of wine, was its main god, and the city was well-known for its many temples. Laodicea, along the Lycus River valley, was fantastically wealthy, being a banking and commercial trading center along with wool processing. The city was also a center of medical studies.

The history of these cities is wrapped up in the overall history of the region. Greeks began to colonize and impact the area at the beginning of the first millennium BCE; by the seventh century, the Lydians represented the greatest power of the area and ruled over most of Asia from Sardis. The Lydians and the entire region fell to the Persians in 549 BCE; despite many insurrections, the Persian yoke was only fully removed in 332 by Alexander the Great. After the "Kingdom of Thrace" and the Attalid rule from Pergamum, Rome finally took over control of the region in 133. Sardis is the oldest of the three; Philadelphia was established by Attalus II in the second century BCE, while Laodicea was founded by the Seleucid Antiochus II in the third century BCE. Despite being a Lydian city, Philadelphia was also known for being a major Hellenistic outpost in Asia.

The area was significantly impacted by earthquakes. Sardis and Philadelphia suffered greatly from an earthquake in 17 CE; even though the cities were rebuilt, Sardis in particular never regained its former glory and importance. Philadelphia, being right on the fault line, suffered recurrent earthquakes for twenty years; they renamed the city Neocaesarea in gratitude to the Roman emperor Tiberius for his financial relief for the city. The great earthquake of 60–61 leveled both Colossae and Laodicea; while Colossae never seemed to recover, Laodicea was fully rebuilt at its

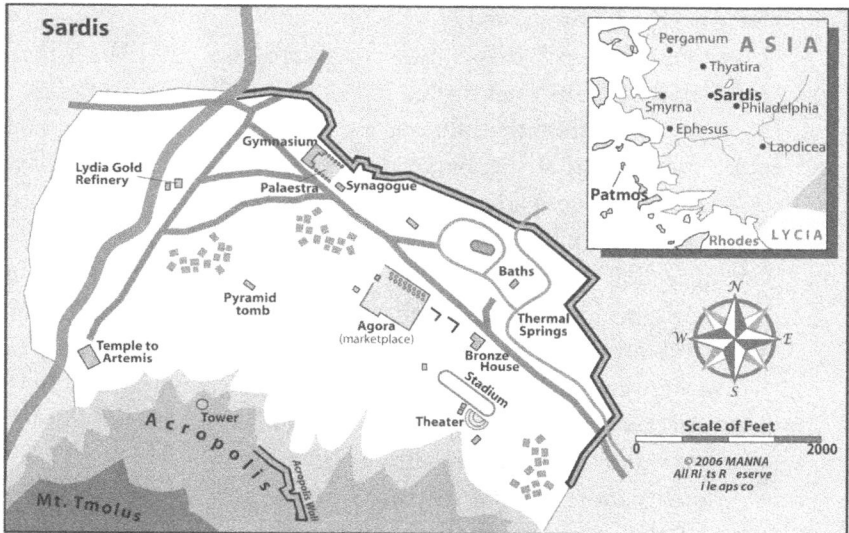

own expense. Such indicates just how much wealth was present in the city in the first century. The situation in Laodicea provides further evidence for a later date of Revelation: the church would have still been recovering in the mid- to late-60s, but would have fully recovered by the 90s.

The Founding of Churches in Asia

The New Testament does not reveal any specific information about how the churches in Sardis or Philadelphia were founded. Laodicea, however, is mentioned in terms of the work of Epaphras in Colossians 4.12–13. It would seem from Colossians 4.16 that Paul even wrote a letter to the church in Laodicea. While some posit that the letter to the Ephesians was actually written to Laodicea, it is more likely that this letter has been lost to us.

Most likely, all three churches were established during Paul's stay in Ephesus (Acts 19.8–10), around 55–57. Their establishment probably followed the same pattern as Colossae and Laodicea: local men, like Epaphras, heard the Gospel from Paul, believed it, and then took it back to the cities in their area. By the 90s, these churches were well-established.

Sardis: The Living Dead

Having spoken to Ephesus, Smyrna, Pergamum, and Thyatira in Revelation 2, Jesus then turned to Sardis in Revelation 3.1–6.

Jesus established that although they have some works and despite the claim that they were alive, they were in fact dead (Rev 3.1). It would seem, then, that there were many in Sardis who professed to be Christians and who professed to be alive to God, but in fact lay in spiritual death (*cf.* Rom 6.3–7, Jas 2.14–26). Jesus continued by establishing that these brethren must strengthen the good intentions that they have, to be watchful. None of their works were complete before God (Rev 3.2). Jesus charged them to repent, returning to what they heard and believed at first, lest He come as a thief and surprise them (Rev 3.3).

The situation of these brethren in Sardis seems further progressed than the situation in Ephesus. These Christians represented the "living dead": they may have good intentions, and they may even progress a little in the faith, but they have nothing complete in God's sight and required significant change if they would be found pleasing to God on the last day. Jesus charged them to change, to return to what was first preached to them, and to be obedient servants of God.

Nevertheless, there were some in Sardis who are faithful; as Jesus says, they have "not defiled their garments," perhaps an oblique reference to the wool garment production of Sardis (Rev 3.4–5). As opposed to those who are "dead," these brethren were "worthy," and "walk[ed] with [Him] in white"; such persons would not be blotted out from the Book of Life, and Jesus would confess them before the Father (Rev 3.4–5).

The church in Sardis is thus a story in contrasts: the faithful brethren who were unstained and walked with Jesus, having their names in the Book of Life, and the unfaithful brethren, dead as they lived, requiring repentance. We can only hope that all were found faithful by God!

Philadelphia: Holding Firm

Jesus then turned to the church in Philadelphia in Revelation

3.7–13. He addressed them as "He who has the key of David" (Rev 3.7) and constantly used the imagery of the open door (possibly a reference to the temples throughout the city?). Jesus spoke in most positive terms of the brethren in Philadelphia: He knew their works, and he knew that they have held to His name and endured in patience (Rev 3.8, 10).

Doors have opened to the Philadelphians, perhaps to promote the Gospel against the "religiosity" of the pagans and Jews among them; Jesus explicitly identified the Jews as a source of trouble, "a synagogue of Satan" like in Smyrna (*cf.* Rev 2.9), who do not honor the God of Israel. Jesus promised that they will be humbled before the brethren in Philadelphia, and God's love for them will be made manifest (Rev 3.9).

The reward for the brethren in Philadelphia was an exemption from the persecution coming to test the earth's inhabitants (Rev 3.10). They were to simply persevere, lest they lose their crown (Rev 3.11). If they endured, they would be part of the New Jerusalem and have the names of God and Christ placed upon them (Rev 3.12).

Such is the end of the New Testament revelation regarding Philadelphia; however, Philadelphia is one of the recipients of letters from Ignatius, "bishop" of Antioch, around 115 CE. Ignatius wrote to the "bishop and elders" of Philadelphia and exhorted the Christians to follow the singular bishop as shepherd (Ignatius, *Letter to the Philadelphians*, 1–2). He warned them about some "schismatics" and dared to assert that "as many as are of God and of Jesus Christ are also with the bishop" (*ibid.* 3); such "schismatics" were to repent and reconcile to the bishop (*ibid.* 8). The Philadelphians were also warned to not accept the Jewish Law (*ibid.* 4, 9).

Thus we see the situation of the church in Philadelphia. Philadelphia was a strong church, considered very faithful to God. Jesus called upon them to endure in the face of Jewish persecution; it seems evident that many of the brethren in Philadelphia were either Jewish or easily affected by Jews, considering the constant Israelite imagery in Jesus' words and Ignatius' need to charge some later not to follow the Jewish law. After the first century, the practice of a bishop having authority over elders was introduced in Philadelphia, and the majority went along with it. It seems just as clear, however, that many disagreed with the practice and were branded as "schismatics"—considered to be divisive persons—for the majority had decreed that the "true practice" was to be in communion with the bishop. This latter end is lamentable; it is a testimony to the strength and stability of the church in Philadelphia, however, that some were willing to protest strongly the innovations brought into that church. We have confidence in the hope that many brethren from Philadelphia will be part of the New Jerusalem on the final day (*cf.* Rev 21).

Laodicea: Consequences of Complacency

The final church addressed by Jesus is Laodicea in Revelation 3.14–22. While all other churches of Asia have at least some positive qualities, none can be found in Laodicea. Jesus began by describing them as "lukewarm," being neither cold nor hot; on account of it, Jesus will spew them from His mouth (Rev 3.15–16). Jesus was not indicating that "hot" is "zealous" and "cold" is "dead"; rather, he used the basic imagery of food or drink: humans do well at handling either hot or cold food and drink—appreciating the heat in cold temperatures and the cold during heat—but lukewarm food and drink is never easily endured. Some believe that Jesus here makes a reference to the water from hot springs brought into the city by a conduit: while it started out hot, it would likely be lukewarm when it reached the city. Regardless, Jesus made it clear that the works of the Laodiceans are less than satisfying and that their salvation is at risk.

The reason for the difficulty is found in Revelation 3.17–18:

> Because thou sayest, "I am rich, and have gotten riches, and have need of nothing;" and knowest not that thou art the wretched one and miserable and poor and blind and naked: I counsel thee to buy of me gold refined by fire, that thou mayest become rich; and white garments, that thou mayest clothe thyself, and that the shame of thy nakedness be not made manifest; and eyesalve to anoint thine eyes, that thou mayest see.

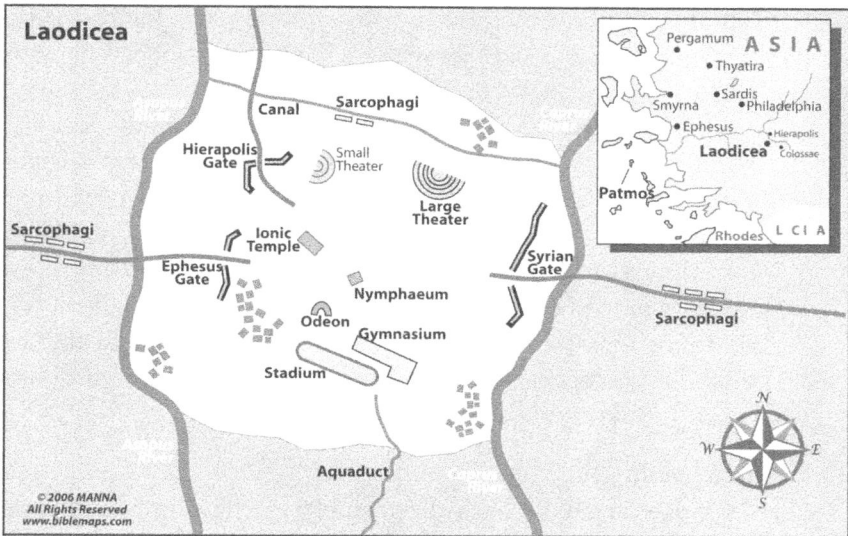

It is clear that the brethren had great wealth; they had many physical blessings, which is consistent with the picture of Laodicea in the first century. Their relative wealth, however, had caused them to become complacent in spiritual matters. Paul charged the rich in this pleasant age not to trust in their riches, but rather to be rich toward God (1 Tim 6.17–19); Laodicea did not follow this advice. Their physical wealth blinded them to their spiritual condition, and as a result, they were found entirely unsatisfying to God.

There was but one thing that the brethren in Laodicea could do: humble themselves, repent, submit to Christ's chastening, and be made spiritually whole and rich. Jesus concludes His warning with the following comfort in Revelation 3.19–21:

> As many as I love, I reprove and chasten: be zealous therefore, and repent. Behold, I stand at the door and knock: if any man hear my voice and open the door, I will come in to him, and will sup with him, and he with me. He that overcometh, I will give to him to sit down with me in my throne, as I also overcame, and sat down with my Father in his throne.

Reproof and chastening is the mark of God's love for the Christian (*cf.* Heb 12.4–13); those who are Christ's will indeed eat with Him and will be with Him forever.

The church in Laodicea provides a sober warning: material abundance can lead to spiritual complacency. It was when the brethren believed that they were "rich" and in need of "nothing" that they were to be cast out by Jesus. The church in Laodicea was so wealthy that they felt as if they needed nothing from Christ; in fact, they needed everything He could offer them. They had been blinded by their wealth from their spiritual depravity, and all they could do was repent or perish. We hope that they indeed did so and will recline with Christ at the end.

Conclusion

Much can be gained from the examples of the churches in Asia. Many churches, like Philadelphia, remain strong despite persecution and are well-grounded in the truth: if the brethren persevere, they will maintain their crowns. Many other churches are like Sardis, having two distinct groups: brethren who are faithful, walking with Christ and doing His will, and other brethren who profess Christianity but do not produce works consistent with that profession. These latter Christians are considered dead as they live and must repent to be found with God on the last day. Too often, however, especially in lands of material abundance, churches like Laodicea are abundant: the members bask in their material resources and confuse material blessings with spiritual significance. While they profess to be great churches, in reality they are pitiable, naked, and destitute. Their material wealth blinds them to their spiritual condition, and if they remain in their complacency, they will be cast out by Jesus. Let us all gain much from the examples of the churches of Asia, heeding what the Spirit says to the churches: let us be faithful to God, wearing unstained garments, overcoming through Jesus (Rev 3).

What God Approves

And whatsoever ye do, in word or in deed, do all in the name of the Lord Jesus, giving thanks to God the Father through him. (Col 3.17)

We have now examined the churches that the New Testament describes in some depth. We have seen where they were located; some of the history of the places; what we can glean from the Scriptures regarding the situation of the churches, their strengths, their struggles; and how they related to themselves and to the apostles. It remains for us to pull all of the disparate pieces together to present a comprehensive picture of the church in the New Testament. Let us begin by considering the positive—what God approved in New Testament churches.

The Church: *Ekklesia*

As Jesus was establishing His body, He established that it should be called the *ekklesia,* the word in Greek used in Matthew 16.18, and then used most consistently to refer to those who are in Christ. The *ekklesia* is further described in terms of its possessor: the *ekklesia* of God (1 Cor 1.2), the *ekklesiai* of Christ (Rom 16.16), and the *ekklesia* of the Firstborn (Heb 12.23). The body is also described as such—the body of Christ (Eph 5.22–33) and the sect of the Nazarenes (Acts 24.5). We therefore see that the *ekklesia* is possessed by God in Christ.

In the New Testament, *ekklesia* is normally translated by the English word "church." This translation is based more on tradition than accuracy; the word *ekklesia* means "assembly" (not "the called out ones," as is often said; *ekklesia derives* from the Greek words meaning "the called out," but such is not the word's *meaning)*. While the English word "church" is appropriate in that it describes a religious collective, the word is otherwise misleading. The *ekklesia* did not refer to a building—as English "church" often does—and an *ekklesia* in Greek need not be highly organized or even religious, even as New Testament use indicates: the riotous mob in Acts 19:32 and the regular political assembly of Ephesus in Acts 19.39 are both called *ekklesiai*, while English "church" has taken on an entirely religious connotation. *Ekklesia* can refer to an actual group of people who have assembled (an "assemblage") or to a group of people with a shared identity, even if that group is not physically together.

Therefore, as we have been talking about the "New Testament church" or "churches of the New Testament," we have spoken about groups described as the *ekklesia* or the *ekklesiai* that belong to Christ. They represent assemblies of persons who came together often in the name of Christ. We understand from the use of the terms that the *ekklesia* has two conceptual references: a "universal" church and a "local" church.

The Nature of the Universal Church

As we have seen, the New Testament often describes the collective of God's people in the new covenant as the "church" (keeping in mind that "church" is defining the Greek *ekklesia)*. Even though the New Testament does not explicitly speak in terms of a "universal church" or a "local church," the way that the terms are used requires this understanding.

For example, in Ephesians 4.4, Paul establishes that there is "one body." In Ephesians 5.22–33, Paul speaks of the church in singular terms, and explicitly defines the body of Christ as the church (Eph 5.29–30). On the other hand, Paul writes to "the church" in Corinth and to "the church" in Thessalonica—even to the "churches" of Galatia (1 Cor 1.2; 1 Thes 1.1, Gal 1.2)! How can there be all of these "churches" if there is only one "church"?

The resolution of this difficulty is the recognition that the church in the New Testament is conceived in terms of both a universal collective and also local collectives. Plenty of ambiguity exists in many passages as to the precise relationship of the two, as we will see in our discussions. Regardless, let us consider what we have seen that God has established regarding the nature of the universal church.

Where the church is spoken of in singular terms, especially in relation to Christ, reference is most often made to the universal church. This is the "church" that Christ establishes in Matthew 16.18. The universal church is most often described in terms of various images relating to Christ: a body (1 Cor 12.12–27), a bride (Rev 21.2, 9), a mix of the two above (Eph 5.23–33), and a temple (Eph 2.19–22).

From this imagery we gain much understanding: the universal church represents those who belong to Christ, who look to Him as their Head. He is knit to the church closely; He died for the church, and the church is now seen as His body. The universal church is envisioned as a collective of individuals working individually, concomitantly, and in local collectives, cleansed through His blood, looking to Jesus as their Lord and Master, striving to do His will.

The temple imagery demonstrates the organization of the universal church (Eph 2.19–22): the church is founded on Jesus Christ as the cornerstone (1 Cor 3.11), who represents its Head/High Priest (Eph 5.23; Heb 9.11). Jesus delegated authority to His apostles, who established the doctrines of the new covenant after His death and therefore also represent part of the foundation of the church (along with the inspired prophets of the day and before; Matt 18.18; John 14.26; 16.7–14; Acts 2). Upon this foundation is built the universal church—its constituent members.

The universal church currently represents an abstract collective that has not yet assembled; it will only have concrete existence on the day of Judgment, when Jesus returns and receives all who are His to Him for eternity (Acts 17.30–31; Matt 25.31–46; 1 Thes 4.14–18). At that point the universal church will be assembled and will remain together for all eternity with its Head who purchased it with His own blood (Ephesians 5:23-33).

The Nature of the Local Church

While the New Testament often speaks of the church as a singular collective, we also see the existence of local collectives of such persons.

As soon as Christianity spread outside of the environs of Jerusalem, disciples were made in many lands. Subsequently, there was the expectation that disciples in a given geographic area were to come together and build one another up (Heb 10.24–25; 1 Cor 14.26). It is not as if Christians still only thought of themselves as belonging to the universal church and just so happened to meet with other such Christians in a given area; the local body is given definition, as we will see, by having elders and deacons established in each such body when able (Acts 14.23). Likewise, Colossians 4.16 indicates the existence of the church on a local level through Paul's ability to tell the "church" in Colossae to read the letter sent to the "church" in Laodicea and vice versa. The local church thus represents those who frequently assemble together in a local area in the name of Christ.

The relationship between the local churches and the universal church is never explicitly defined. It is clear enough that the ideal was that the local church would represent a manifestation of the collective of all of the living members of the universal church in a given geographic area—no more, no less. On the other hand, the fact that the New Testament indicates that there were people present in local churches who would not be part of the saved shows how this reality is not precisely met (*cf.* 1 Cor 5; Rev 2–3). While many of the metaphors described above have reference to the universal church, their practical function is most often realized in the local churches. For instance, the idea of the church as a body—with each member as a part of a greater whole, each bringing in their own abilities and working together with other such persons—may abstractly refer to the universal church, but the actual working together, encouragement, building up, *etc.* mentioned in the passage are realized by the brethren in Corinth working together themselves (1 Cor 12.12–27). While it is clear that Christians are to love brethren outside of their local church

(1 Thes 4.9–10), the joint participation in Christianity will always be most realized by the Christians in the local church, with whom the Christian is to constantly assemble (Heb 10.25). The ambiguity is present perhaps to point to the ideal and also to account for the reality that when Jesus returns, there will no longer be any local churches, but only the one universal church.

The Christian should therefore be a part of Christ's universal church while also being identified with a local church of brethren of like faith (Col 1.18–23; 1 Cor 1.10; 1 John 1.6–7). Such a Christian is to be held accountable to his fellow brethren in the local church (1 Cor 5; Gal 6.2); such indicates the need for Christians to explicitly identify themselves with a local body of Christ's people.

God established specific organization for local churches. The head of every church is Christ (Rom 16.16; 1 Cor 1.2). The apostles also represent authorities in local churches, if not in person, then through devotion to their teachings (Eph 2.19–22; Acts 2.42). God also established elders (also called overseers and shepherds) in every local church as able and where men meet certain qualifications to be such (Acts 14.23; 1 Pet 5.1–4; 1 Thes 1.1; 1 Tim 3.1–8; Tit 1.5–7). These men are directed to guide and oversee the local church according to God's standards and will be held responsible for their oversight (1 Pet 5.1–4; Heb 13.17). Deacons also were appointed (again, where men meet certain qualifications) to serve the local church (1 Tim 3.9–12). Within the church one may find evangelists promoting God's truth and teachers explaining the same (Eph 4.11); such persons have no intrinsic authority beyond the need to observe the word of God as it is properly set forth. All those baptized believers in Christ who identify themselves as part of the local church represent its members (Acts 2.47); their responsibilities will be set forth below.

Local churches thus represent the functional concepts of the church that will continue as long as the earth remains. At the Judgment, when Jesus returns to gather His own, every local church will be dissolved. Those who truly belong to Christ will be gathered together into the universal church, as established above. In idealistic terms, local churches represent collectives of the saved in various geographic areas, shepherded by elders and served by deacons, constantly assembling together.

The Constituency of the Church

By necessity of what has been established above from Ephesians 5.22–33, 1 Thessalonians 4.14–18, and other passages, we may see that the universal church is composed of all of the individuals who are saved under the new covenant between God and mankind through Christ Jesus and who are known to Him (Matt 7.21–23; Heb 9; Rev 21).

The local church is constituted of Christians in a given area who have association with one another on the basis of their joint walk with Christ and who assemble together frequently (1 John 1.6–7; Heb 10.24–25). The assemblies may also include the children of such Christians and perhaps other interested persons. Ideally, as established, all members of the local church will also be members of the universal church.

The church, therefore, is composed of people. The life and conduct of these people find constant address, especially in the letters of the New Testament. The expectation exists that all such individuals are to be obedient servants of God (Rom 6.16–23). This obedience is represented in many ways. Christians are to engage in moral conduct, manifesting the fruit of the Spirit (Gal 5.17–24). Christians are to help those who are in need, especially those in the household of the faith (Gal 6.10). Christians are expected to fulfill God's plan for their lives in every aspect: old and young, man and woman, husband and wife, parent and child, master (employer) and slave (employee), and of course as fellow Christians (Tit 2; Eph 5.22–6.9; 1 Tim 5.1–2). They are to love their fellow man, humbly considering the good of his or her neighbor over his or her own good, and always be ready and willing to promote the Gospel of Christ, defending the hope with gentleness and respect (Matt 19.19; Phil 2.1–4; Matt 28.18–20; Rom 1.16–17; 1 Pet 3.15–16). Where there are elders, Christians are to be subject to them

(Heb 13.17). The Christian, therefore, is to be a disciple of Christ, striving to fulfill (and be seen in light of) Galatians 2.20:

> I have been crucified with Christ; and it is no longer I that live, but Christ living in me: and that life which I now live in the flesh I live in faith, the faith which is in the Son of God, who loved me, and gave himself up for me.

The individual Christian is part of the church universal and a local church, having many responsibilities toward his fellow brethren; nevertheless, the Christian also has a life outside of the assembly and is called upon to present him or herself as a child of light in a dark world (Matt 5.13–16). The church is composed of people; the individual people have functions both as individuals and in joint participation with others in the faith.

Functions of the Church

Since the universal church currently represents an abstract concept, its function is represented more in terms of the local church, as described below. The existence of the universal church helps us to realize that we are all part of something greater than the local church, and the reality of the universal church ties all true believers together in Christ Jesus (Eph 5.22–33). The full function of the universal church awaits the return of Jesus and the resurrection when that body will be assembled for eternity (Rev 21).

The functions of the local church are manifest in Ephesians 4.16:

> From whom all the body fitly framed and knit together through that which every joint supplieth, according to the working in due measure of each several part, maketh the increase of the body unto the building up of itself in love.

All of the functions of the local church embody the principle of increasing the body through building up itself in love.

Edification

As established in Ephesians 4.16, one major aspect of the function of the church, especially in the local church, is edification—the building up of itself in love. We see the following in Hebrews 10.24–25:

> And let us consider one another to provoke unto love and good works; not forsaking our own assembling together, as the custom of some is, but exhorting one another; and so much the more, as ye see the day drawing nigh.

The author of Hebrews indicates the need for Christians to consider how to stir one another up to love and to have good works and further indicates the role of the assembly in these matters. While the church can be edified in some ways outside of the assembly, the regular assemblies of the saints represent the constant and consistent venue in which Christians may build one another up and therefore build up the church in love.

Christians assembled on many occasions to build one another up (Acts 2.46; 1 Cor 14.26). We see that Christians met on the first day of the week to break bread, most likely a way of speaking of the Lord's Supper, and also to have a collection for the financial needs of the church (Acts 20.7; 1 Cor 16.16). On these occasions, a lesson would be preached (Acts 20.7); no doubt, Christians would have also had prayers of thanksgiving (1 Cor 14.14–17) and would have sung psalms, hymns, and spiritual songs, speaking, teaching, and admonishing one another with their messages (Eph 5.19; Col 3.16). These assemblies were to be orderly and peaceful (1 Cor 14.33; 1 Tim 2.8). It is likely that Christians also spent time in these assemblies devoting themselves to the apostles' doctrines and the entire Word of God (Acts 2.42). There are examples of brethren assembling for spiritual purposes beyond the first day of the week (Acts 2.46); Christians certainly came together for prayers, singing, teaching, and preaching on other opportunities than just on the first day of the week.

Such represents the times of spiritual assembly; Christians also came together for shared meals (Acts 2.46; 1 Pet 4.9). The New Testament presupposes that Christians love one another, spend time together, know each other like family members, and are able to be there for one another in good times and bad (Phil 2.1–4;

Rom 12.10, Gal 6.1–2). The members of the local church are to care for one another:

> That there should be no schism in the body; but that the members should have the same care one for another. And whether one member suffereth, all the members suffer with it; or one member is honored, all the members rejoice with it. (1 Cor 12.25–26)

As we have seen, the love of the brethren has made all the difference among churches of the New Testament: it can make all the difference between being like the church in Thessalonica and being like the church in Corinth (*cf.* 1 Thes 4.9). Indeed, this love for brethren should extend beyond the local church to all Christians, as seen in 1 Thessalonians 4.9–10, but will it always be most fully realized in the midst of the Christians with whom one constantly assembles. Always considering how to encourage and edify one another, such brethren will lead to the church being edified and thus following the will of God.

Benevolence

Building up in love is not restricted only to spiritual benefit—when called upon, the local church is to provide for Christians in physical need. The church in Antioch provided relief for the Christians in Judea when a famine occurred (Acts 11.29–30); the churches of Macedonia and Achaia provided similar relief for a later need (Rom 15.26; 2 Cor 8–9). Paul counseled Timothy regarding the support for "widows indeed" in Ephesus, expecting the church to provide physical support for those Christian widows who had no other means of assistance (1 Tim 5.5–10). While being expected to take care of their own (1 Tim 5.8, 16), Christians could also support brethren in need from the collective resources and were encouraged strongly to do so when the need arose.

Evangelism

Building up the body in love involves both strengthening those who already constitute the church and supporting the work to add to the number of the church. The Lord ordained that they who proclaim the Gospel should live by the Gospel (1 Cor 9.14);

elders who both shepherded and labored in the Word were worthy of double honor and payment (1 Tim 5.18–19). Antioch is especially noted for their focus on the promotion of the Gospel, willingly sending out Paul and Barnabas to preach in Cyprus and Asia Minor (Acts 13.1–3). Churches like Philippi supported Paul even when Paul was preaching in other places (Phil 4.15–18). Acts 19.19 may indicate that many of the disciples were active in the preaching of the Word with Paul and that much of what was accomplished was done by collective effort. By all means the local churches worked to empower and encourage its constituent members to promote the Gospel in their own lives, fulfilling the divine mandate (Matt 28.18–20).

The functions of the church, especially as manifest in the local churches, represent the need to build up the Body; the collective work is always focused on the building up of the collective, be it through encouragement in the assembly, providing support for its members, or promoting the Gospel to increase its size. When Christians devoted themselves to the building up of the body in love, the local church was strengthened and grew into maturity.

Conclusion

We have seen, in large part, what the New Testament indicates that God approves in terms of the church, its nature, its constituency, and its function. Let us all strive to do that which is pleasing to God to the building up of the body in love and the salvation of souls!

What God Condemns

Be not ye therefore partakers with them; For ye were once darkness, but are now light in the Lord: walk as children of light (for the fruit of the light is in all goodness and righteousness and truth), proving what is well-pleasing unto the Lord; and have no fellowship with the unfruitful works of darkness, but rather even reprove them; for the things which are done by them in secret it is a shame even to speak of. (Eph 5.7–12)

We have previously examined the individual churches of the New Testament and are now attempting to gain the larger picture of God's intentions for the church in the New Testament. To this end, we have recognized that which God approved for the church in the New Testament; let us now continue with an analysis of what God condemned in the church in the New Testament.

Sin
In short, we can say that God condemned sin in the churches of the New Testament, as is written in Romans 14.23 and 1 John 3.4–6:

> But he that doubteth is condemned if he eat, because he eateth not of faith; and whatsoever is not of faith is sin.

> Every one that doeth sin doeth also lawlessness; and sin is lawlessness. And ye know that he was manifested to take away sins; and in him is no sin. Whosoever abideth in him sinneth not: whosoever sinneth hath not seen him, neither knoweth him.

That which is not according to faith—that which springs up from lawlessness, teachings not established from God, and so forth—is sin, and unrepentant sin has no place in the church of the New Testament (Eph 5.22–33).

"Sin" is itself a broad category; the New Testament provides many lists of such sins, including Galatians 5.19–21:

> Now the works of the flesh are manifest, which are these: fornication, uncleanness, lasciviousness, idolatry, sorcery, enmities, strife, jealousies, wraths, factions, divisions, parties, envyings, drunkenness, revellings, and such like; of which I forewarn you, even as I did forewarn you, that they who practise such things shall not inherit the kingdom of God.

While most of these sins involve the individual Christian, the impact of an individual's sin on the church can be significant indeed; much of what was written to the churches of the New Testament regarded the conduct of their constituent members. A church represents the collective of its constituent individuals; their inappropriate conduct could occur within the context of their individual lives or in the context of the assembly. Let us consider these sins in more depth, especially as they relate to the churches of the New Testament.

Sexual Sin

The first three "works of the flesh" mentioned in Galatians 5.19–21 are forms of sexual sin: sexually deviant behavior, uncleanness, and lasciviousness. Matters of sexual sin are often found at the top of such lists: then as now, misdirected sexual desire has led many to commit sin. The Roman world in which the Christians lived was more tolerant of many sexual practices that God considered sin; one of the great challenges, especially among the Gentile brethren, was the elimination of such sin from their midst (Acts 15.20; 29; 1 Cor 6.15–20; Eph 4.17–19; 1 Thes 4.1–7).

Sexually deviant behavior (Greek *porneia*, translated also as "fornication" or "sexual immorality") is the term most often used to describe such sexual sin and is found in many of the lists of sin (Matt 15.19/Mark 7.21; 1 Cor 6.9; Gal 5.19; Eph 5.3; Col 3.5). Paul shows great concern with sexually deviant behavior, encouraging brethren to flee from it (1 Cor 6.18). He recognized that sexual sin is easily rationalized, since it does not "hurt" anyone else; nevertheless, it is a sin against one's own body, which is to be the temple of the Holy Spirit (1 Cor 6.18–20).

Sexually deviant behavior includes any form of deviant actions involving some other creature. Adultery—sex with another man or woman other than one's spouse—is included (cf. Matt 19.9; Rom 13.9). Such was the fruit of the doctrine of the Nicolaitans, which Jesus hated (Rev 2.6, 15–16); if Jesus speaks literally regarding the sins of "Jezebel" in Thyatira, she is guilty of the same and its promotion (Rev 2.20). Visitation of prostitutes would also be included, be it either adultery or fornication (1 Cor 6.15–17). Sexually deviant behavior also includes incest and incest-like relations; the man "who had his father's wife" in 1 Corinthians 5 was to be "delivered over to Satan" for his conduct. Strict fornication—sexual activity before marriage—is likewise included (cf. 1 Cor 7.2–3). Homosexuality is also sexually deviant behavior, an unnatural object of passion (Rom 1.26–27; 1 Cor 6.9–10). Bestiality, pedophilia, and other such behaviors would also be included. It is understandable why Paul would spend so much time warning brethren about these things!

Uncleanness is the result of such sexual deviancy—there is a sense of defiling when one commits improper sexual action (the word can refer to lack of physical cleanliness, but is most often used in a sexual context; cf. Rom 1.24; 6.19; 2 Cor 12.21; Eph 5.3; Col 3.5; 1 Thes 2.3; 4.7). It is not merely sexual conduct that causes concern; lust and lustful actions that would precipitate sexual misconduct also fall under condemnation, as does lasciviousness (Mark 7.22; Rom 13.13; 2 Cor 12.21; Gal 5.19; Eph 4.13; 1 Pet 4.3, 2 Pet 2.7, 18; Jude 1.4; cf. Matt 5.28).

Sexual deviancy and its promotion are clearly condemned in the New Testament, and many churches of the New Testament suffered on account of the sexual misdeeds of some of their members. Such demonstrates the need to esteem marriage properly and to exhort all Christians to keep sexual conduct within its bounds (1 Cor 7.1–5; Heb 13.4).

Idolatry and Sorcery

The next "works of the flesh" involve trusting in powers other than God: idolatry and sorcery. Idolatry was a constant problem in the Old Testament for Israel and remained a temptation in the days of the New Testament; on a concrete level, idolatry involved the creation of an image, the declaration that the image represented a deity, and the veneration of that image. The Christian should recognize that an idol is really nothing (1 Cor 8); regardless, idolatry is condemned often (1 Cor 5.10–11; 6.9–10; 10.7; 10.14; 12.2; 2 Cor 6.16; Gal 5.20; 1 Pet 4.3; 1 John 5.21).

Idolatry involved more than just concrete images. Paul condemns covetousness as "idolatry" in Ephesians 5.3, 5 and Colossians 3.5. This is consistent with Jesus' warning in Matthew 6.24: one cannot serve both God and "mammon," which represents a god of riches. Covetousness itself was condemned in the Ten Commandments given to Israel (Exod 20.17), and that command was also established in the new covenant (Mark 7.22; Luke 12.15; Rom 1.29; 13.9; 1 Cor 5.10–11; Jas 4.2; 2 Pet 2.14). The desire for riches is a root of all kind of evil (1 Tim 6.9–10), and God's people should flee from it (1 Tim 6.11). One need only see the example of Ananias and Sapphira to see the consequences of such greed (Acts 5.1–11)!

Sorcery represents the "black arts," including necromancy, psychic powers, and the like. Those who trust in God should not turn to such powers.

Idolatry was an especially great concern in many churches, since so many Gentiles had come out of an idolatrous past and could perhaps be led back into it (*cf.* 1 Cor 8). All Christians are to be exhorted to put their trust in the living God.

Interpersonal Relations

Many of the "works of the flesh" condemned by God represent misconduct in interpersonal relations and improper thoughts and perspectives regarding others: enmity, strife, jealousy, wrath, rivalry, and envy.

Enmity is the hatred of others. John indicates clearly that no one can love God and yet hate his brother (1 John 4.20); hatred, therefore, ought not to be named among saints (Gal 5.20).

Strife and rivalry are similar words in Greek and represent similar difficulties, especially within a local church. They refer to contention, displays of discord among groups of persons, and a factious spirit. Such should not mark the Christian (Rom 1.29; 2.8; 13.13; Phil 2.13; 1 Tim 6.4; Tit 3.9; Jas 3.14, 16). Diotrephes in 3 John 9–10 has all the markings of a factious man, desiring preeminence and unjustly casting those brethren who disagree with him out of the church. The church in Corinth was especially known for its contentiousness, factiousness, and internal strife, all of which were roundly condemned by Paul (1 Cor 1.10–16; 3.3; 11.16–34; 2 Cor 12.20). Strife and disputes, therefore, were among the great difficulties in some New Testament churches.

Jealousy and envy are similar concepts. Both involve an inordinate desire for possession: jealousy exists when one actually possesses the object and zealously protects it, and envy exists when one does not possess the object but greatly desires to do so. They can refer to people, stations in life, or actual material things. Both are condemned in the New Testament (*jealousy:* Rom 13.13; Gal 5.20; Jas 3.14; 16; *envy:* Rom 1.29; Gal 5.21; Phil 1.15; 1 Tim 6.4; Tit 3.3; 1 Pet 2.1). The spirit of jealousy plagued Corinth also and perhaps in no small measure led to the strife there (1 Cor 3.3; 2 Cor 12.20). The internal suspicions engendered by jealousy and envy have no room in the church, for they serve to tear down rather than to build up.

Wrath and outbursts of anger represent a lack of self-control and can lead to great destruction. One can be angry without sin (Eph 4.26). Nevertheless, anger out of control is to be put away (2 Cor 12.20; Gal 5.20; Eph 4.31; Col 3.8), and not used to destroy the brethren (or anyone, for that matter) who require building up.

Much hostility, strife, jealousy, envy, and anger are engendered from other forms of sin condemned in the New Testament. Churches of the New Testament seemed to have difficulties with some members, especially widows and the unemployed, being busybodies and gossips (2 Thes 3.11; 1 Tim 5.13). Such discussions did not lead to the building up of the hearers, but led many to be led astray by Satan (1 Tim 5.14–15). Lying to one another also would pose a difficulty, and Paul urges Christians to do no such thing (Col 3.9–11). It is imperative, then, that Christians work, not spread gossip, and be honest with one another, for not a little difficulty has been caused in churches by such behavior.

Dissensions and Heresies: Fruit of False Teaching

While many would profess that what one believes or what one teaches may not necessarily matter, God neither accepts nor establishes any such thing in the New Testament. The promulgation of false teaching is condemned as sin, with dissensions and heresies representing works of the flesh just like sexual deviant behavior or drunkenness.

The results of false teaching and the acceptance of false teachers are clear from the pages of the New Testament. The "Judaizing" controversy—whether the Law of Moses was to be bound upon Gentiles—is first seen in Antioch, having come from Jerusalem (Acts 15.1–3), and would later lead to internal strife in Antioch (Gal 2.11–14). These false teachers attempted to lead the Galatians astray, and Paul chided them strongly for accepting a false gospel that is accursed, warning them about falling away from Christ, even to the point of desiring the emasculation of those who taught the doctrines (Gal 1.6–9; 5.1–4; 5.12)! Similar teachers entered Corinth and turned many of the brethren against Paul, precipitating the need for his second letter to the Corinthians and a visit by Paul to Corinth (2 Cor 11–13). Paul writes harsh words regarding such "Judaizers" in Philippians 3.2–6 and warns the Colossians against observing Jewish scruples in Colossians 2.12–17. Such influences even provide difficulties at the end of the century with Philadelphia in Revelation 3.9. Jewish myths, stories, and genealogies also presented difficulties for Timothy in Ephesus (1 Tim 1.3–8; 4.7). All such teachings led to contention, strife, and no doubt the loss of some souls.

Incipient Gnosticism also wreaked havoc among the churches. Gnostics, who professed superior "knowledge" (Greek *gnosis*), did not believe that Jesus was really God in the flesh, but merely seemed to be that way, and also developed many other doctrines diverging from the truth. Paul must warn the Colossians about falling prey to such worldly philosophies in Colossians 2.4–10, and he warns Timothy against such "knowledge" in 1 Timothy 6.20–21. It is possible that Hymenaeus and Philetus fell away on account of such Gnostic teachings (2 Tim 2.16–18). Concern regarding Gnostics is prevalent in the book of John, in which John constantly emphasizes that Jesus came in the flesh and the imperative to not accept those who teach to the contrary (1 John 4.2; 2 John 7–10). Such contrary teachers were the "antichrists" of the day (1 John 2.18–23).

False teachings, false teachers, and immoral conduct are often wrapped together in the New Testament: many times, they follow each other. Paul in 1 Timothy 6.3–8 and 2 Timothy 4.3–4, Peter in 2 Peter 2, and Jude in Jude 1.4–19 all speak of false teachers, those who accept such false teachers, and their immorality. Nothing but evil is gained from such exploits.

The authors of the New Testament sadly look forward to the times of apostasy and "falling away" that would take place. Paul laments such things in Acts 20.29–30, 2 Thessalonians 2.3, 1 Timothy 4.1–3, and 2 Timothy 4.3-4.

It is manifest, then, that false teachings posed as much of a problem for the churches of the New Testament as immorality did. Paul considers both immorality and false teaching as "leavening" the lump (1 Cor 5.6; Gal 5.9). Christians must be on guard, not just for improper practice, but also improper thought, belief, and teaching (2 Cor 10.5)!

Excess and Riot

Other works of the flesh involve excess and riotous behavior: drunkenness and revelry (Gal 5.21). Drunkenness—being intoxicated with alcohol—is often condemned in the Scriptures (Luke 21.34; Rom 13.13; Gal 5.21); it is contrary to sobriety, an essential part of the Christian's walk (1 Pet 4.7). Revelry (the party life) represents the same, things done by Gentiles and not by Christians (Rom 13.13; Gal 5.21, 1 Pet 4.3).

Paul also warns Christians to avoid "things like" the works of the flesh (Gal 5.19–21). Anything that concords, then, with the works of the flesh and is contrary to the fruit of the Spirit should be avoided and condemned. Christians should not desire to "toe the line" of sin, but stay as far away from it as possible (*cf.* 1 Cor 6.18).

Good Things Used Sinfully

In the New Testament, sin is not confined to only that which is intrinsically wrong. Romans 14 and 1 Corinthians 8 indicate that legitimate liberties, if used improperly, can lead to sin.

Romans 14 represents Paul's response to contention present within the church in Rome. Evidently there were some brethren who believed in the liberty to eat any kind of meat and not to observe days; other brethren did not believe in the liberty to eat meat and observed specific days (Rom 14.2–5). Paul definitively establishes that such liberties are of no concern to God; as matters of "food and drink," they do not infringe on the "righteousness, peace, and joy of the Holy Spirit" (Rom 14.17) and should not lead to such disputation. All things are clean of themselves, but they are unclean to the one who believes them to be unclean (Rom 14.14). The brethren are encouraged not to put a stumbling block in a brother's way (Rom 14.13) and not to let the good be spoken of as evil (Rom 14.16). Christians should not destroy with food "him for whom Christ died" (Rom 14.15). Matters of liberty should not be used as sources of contentiousness or division, lest they become sin.

First Corinthians 8 presents another situation: some Christians use the liberty of eating meat sacrificed to idols, knowing that there really is no such thing (1 Cor 8.1–6). There were other brethren, however, who had not yet reached that understanding, and the example of the "stronger" brethren might lead them to believe that it is legitimate to eat meat sacrificed to an idol in honor of the idol (1 Cor 8.7). Paul urges the brethren in Corinth to exhibit love, not the arrogance of knowledge, and to be willing to sacrifice the liberty so that their fellow brethren will not stumble (1 Cor 8.8–13). The "weak" should not perish on account of their "knowledge" (1 Cor 8.11), and to do so is not only to sin against them, but even to sin against Christ (1 Cor 8.12). More mature knowledge is thus no excuse for causing a less mature Christian to stumble.

We can see, therefore, that Christians must exercise care even in legitimate matters of liberty, lest they cause their brethren to stumble. Christians are not to act so as to have their good things be spoken of in evil ways.

New Testament Churches' Response to Sin

We have seen the types of sin that God condemned in New Testament churches. Most of the sins involved are of a personal and individual nature; nevertheless, such matters required the attention of the entire group. Any sin without repentance can condemn (Heb 10.26–31); Christians must be marked by continual confession and repentance of sin (1 John 1.8–9). If any Christian is found to be in unrepentant sin, such represents a problem not only for that individual, but also for the local church of which he is a part. Christ's church must be cleansed by His blood; there can be no such stain of sin (Eph 5.26–27). Association of brethren in Christ is fully dependent on a shared walk with Christ in the light (1 John 1.6–7). If anyone is not walking in that light, Christians walking in the light cannot maintain spiritual association with them!

It is manifest why sins involving the assembly would be of great importance to the church; it should also be clear that matters of individual sin without repentance would equally cause difficulty. The New Testament provides instruction in these matters: Matthew 18.15–18 demonstrates how a brother in sin should be handled, first being approached by one, then by a few brethren, and then before the whole church. If he does not repent, he should be treated as a tax-collector or a Gentile. Romans 16.17–18 encourages brethren to avoid those who cause contention or teach that which is false; Timothy was to avoid those who taught error (1 Tim 6.3–11), and John says that Christians should not show hospitality or even greet such persons (2 John 1.10–11). Those caught up in immorality are to be handled in similar ways: 1 Corinthians 5 indicates that Christians caught up in sin should be delivered over to Satan, disfellowshipped from the local church; 2 Thessalonians 3.14–15 indicates that those who do not pay attention to the instructions of Paul should be noted and avoided—not to be treated as enemies, but admonished as brothers.

Such acts of distancing and disassociation served two functions: they indicated to the one sinning that their actions were unacceptable, and the separation would hopefully compel them to repent; it also sent a message to everyone in the church, demonstrating that sin would not be tolerated because the lump is not to be leavened (1 Cor 5.6; Gal 5.9). Such should indicate to all the seriousness of sin and the great importance that should be placed on avoiding that which God condemns!

The New Testament Church

Husbands, love your wives, even as Christ also loved the church, and gave himself up for it; that he might sanctify it, having cleansed it by the washing of water with the word, that he might present the church to himself a glorious church, not having spot or wrinkle or any such thing; but that it should be holy and without blemish. (Eph 5.25–27)

We have now examined the churches of the New Testament. We began where the church began in Jerusalem, seeing its extraordinary beginnings and tragic end. We then followed the expansion of the church to Antioch, a multi-ethnic and evangelistically-minded group, and then to the churches of Galatia, who started well and yet fell prey to false teachings. Philippi and Thessalonica were hard ground for the Gospel (leading to Paul's quick departure), yet the churches quickly matured in love. The churches in Corinth and Ephesus were blessed with Paul's presence for a long time, but both churches manifested internal difficulties. The churches of Rome and Colossae were bereft of apostles at their beginnings; Rome grew strong while Colossae suffered from internal sectarianism. The churches of Asia in Revelation—Smyrna, Pergamum, Thyatira, Sardis, Philadelphia, and Laodicea—were different bodies with differing strengths and weaknesses, often suffering persecution from without and other difficulties within.

We then established, on the basis of what is revealed in the New Testament, what God approved and condemned in the New Testament church—His expectations for that body and those who would comprise it.

It remains for us to return to the questions that we asked in the introduction to our journey, to consider what we have learned, and to do our best to answer them: can we discern the "New Testament church"? Is there even such a thing? Does it represent a monolithic structure, or is it manifest in different groups? Can we speak of a "New Testament church" or only "New Testament churches"? In the end, is the picture of the church in the New Testament coherent or paradigmatic?

The New Testament Church: An Ideal

Perhaps one of the clearest themes found in the study of New Testament churches is the variety of churches described and the many differences among them. No two churches mentioned are the same: each has its own mix of strengths and weaknesses, successes and problems. How can we find any kind of coherence in this diversity?

When we established that which God approved in the New Testament church, we highlighted the reality that much of what is said regarding the church is established in the ideal. In the ideal, the local church will manifest the presently living members of the universal church in a given area. In the ideal, the members of a local church will work together in harmony. In the ideal, each and every member will live up to the conduct expected of them throughout the New Testament.

Likewise, in the ideal, a given church will manifest the characteristics that marked the New Testament church, and all Christians everywhere in all local churches would also manifest those characteristics. Paul wrote in 1 Corinthians 4.7:

> For this cause have I sent unto you Timothy, who is my beloved and faithful child in the Lord, who shall put you in remembrance of my ways which are in Christ, even as I teach everywhere in every church.

Paul did not vary in what he preached. He did not preach one thing in Antioch, another thing in Corinth, and a third thing in Rome; he preached the same message everywhere in every church.

The way in which the message was preached may vary, but what he focused upon and which situations needed addressing would also be different. Nevertheless, the same Gospel was preached, and if the same Gospel was not preached, Paul would be accursed by his own saying (Gal 1.6–9)!

Just as there is an ideal in conduct, there is an ideal in terms of the church. As we have investigated the churches of the New Testament, we have seen that the majority of the variations among the churches were not in regards to matters approved by God, but rather those which God condemned. There was no toleration of the Galatians accepting circumcision from the "Judaizers." There was a full expectation that the factiousness and contention in Corinth were to end. Jesus constantly stresses to many of the churches in Revelation the need to change their ways lest they perish. Regardless, love for the brethren, proper godly conduct, establishment of elders and deacons in each local church, *etc.*, were expected in every church, be it Rome, Corinth, Antioch, or anywhere else.

Tragically, we humans cannot reach the ideal; we all continually fall short of the glory of God, and we sin (Rom 3.23; 1 John 1.8). Since the constituent members of the church are thus imperfect, local churches are also imperfect. Even the strongest, most mature churches in the New Testament could still grow, develop, and improve (1 Thes 4.1, 9). More sin can always be avoided; more love and goodwill can always be generated.

It is legitimate, therefore, to speak of the "New Testament church." The New Testament church represents the ideal that God has set for the church as revealed in the New Testament, embodying all of the positive characteristics and none of the negative ones that we found in New Testament churches. It is the goal to which all churches should aspire.

Churches or Denominations?

We recognize that the "New Testament church" represents an ideal: how do churches operate in practical, real terms?

This question takes on even more significance in our own day than it perhaps did in previous years. In the world of "Christendom," we have seen the rise of ecumenism, espousing the belief that multiple "Christian" denominations—each teaching its own specific doctrines—still can collectively represent the "Christian church" or the "Church of Christ." In an attempt to rationalize this perspective, many of ecumenicalism's adherents turn to the New Testament and portray the local churches as separate denominations. "Corinth" is reckoned as a denomination, as are "Philippi," "Thessalonica," and "Ephesus." All of these "denominations" are considered part of the universal church.

We must portray the nature of the churches of the New Testament accurately. Do the individual churches represent denomination-like structures, or do they represent localized groups of people accepting the same doctrines and practices, striving to represent the ideal?

Much of the argumentation to support the denominational hypothesis focuses on the variety found in churches in the New Testament in belief and practice. Nevertheless, as we have seen, the variety is not based on what is approved. Sure, Corinth does not seem to have elders; that may say more about the lack of fitness of the men in Corinth than it does the idea that they have an intentionally different form of organization, as, say, Presbyterians differ from Methodists. Paul desired to establish elders in every church (Acts 14.23; Tit 1.5). Likewise, Paul desired that the same truth be taught in every church: he personally taught the same Gospel wherever he went (1 Cor 4.17) and declared as anathema, or accursed, any other Gospel (Gal 1.6–9).

It is often believed that since the denominational world agrees on the "essentials," the other matters may be considered "liberties," akin to what is seen in Romans 14. We should note, however, that Romans 14 does not indicate that different structures should exist; the brethren should work together despite differences in matters of liberty and not maintain different churches in Rome! Regardless, the argument begs the question: are the differences among, say, Calvinists and Arminians, Lutherans and Baptists, and so on and so forth, merely matters of "food and drink"? If Paul sharply condemned the Galatians for accepting circumcision and warned the Colossians about both Jewish and Hellenistic intrusion, can we really say that whether God predetermines one's salvation, the role of baptism in salvation, or any one of a multitude of issues are merely matters of liberty?

Paul desired that Christians be "united in the same mind and judgment" (1 Cor 1.10; Phil 2.1–4). This was expected to extend beyond the borders of a local church. In the New Testament, we do not see different churches having different forms of hierarchy, structure, and organization, having "unity in diversity" as it is often touted today, or representing different denominational groups. This hypothesis is not derived from New Testament teachings but instead is being imposed upon it.

From our study, we have established that the apostles and others went about preaching the Gospel, with local churches being established where the message bore fruit. The same message was preached in every place. One *should* hear the same messages being preached in Corinth and Ephesus, Rome and Jerusalem, Sardis and Antioch. These groups were not perfect, and there were some matters concerning which disagreement was tolerable. They represent imperfect groups striving to manifest God's ideal, not complacent denominational structures.

A Coherent Church or Paradigmatic Churches?

When we began our study, we asked whether the New Testament would reveal a coherent New Testament church or provide views of different churches that would serve as patterns or paradigms for later local churches. Let us return to this question.

As we have seen, we can speak of a coherent New Testament church in the ideal. There is not one church in the New Testament that fully manifested that ideal. Neither has any church since been able to achieve it perfectly, since all churches consist of imperfect people. Nevertheless, there is a goal to which all should aspire. Local churches should aspire to manifest the New Testament church, doing all that God has approved and avoiding all that God has condemned.

It should be noted that the goal is not to have "cookie cutter" churches, for each individual local church will be made up of different individuals with different talents and abilities, bringing different things to the table. This is not only expected, but is encouraged in the New Testament, as we have seen in Romans 12 and 1 Corinthians 12. The diversity of individuals, however, does not change the fact that all are expected to hold to the same Gospel and conduct themselves accordingly. Christians can be united in mind and judgment and still be different people!

Nevertheless, we should not so quickly dismiss the value of the churches of the New Testament as individual case studies or "paradigms." With sober judgment (*cf.* 2 Cor 13.5), members of local churches should consider their strengths and weaknesses and compare themselves to what is seen in the New Testament. While a local church will rarely will find its exact equivalent in the New Testament, a local church can find valuable insight from considering what was required from their New Testament cousins. A "Philippian" or "Thessalonian" church can see that they should continue to persevere in what they are doing and do so even more. An "Ephesian" church needs to re-establish itself in the Gospel. Not a few churches are like those in Revelation: few can deny the parallels between Sardis and many churches today, and too many may end up like Laodicea. While we should never have "tunnel vision" and focus exclusively on the portrayal of one church in the New Testament, we can gain considerable insight in understanding how God would desire a given church to grow by looking at what He said to the various churches of the New Testament.

In the end, the New Testament indicates the value in seeing the church both in terms of a coherent whole—the ideal New Testament church—and also in terms of the local New Testament churches, each with its own struggles and successes, strengths and weaknesses. Let us all strive for the ideal, being found obedient servants of God, part of His church for all eternity.

Timeline

5–4* BCE	Birth of Jesus
27–30 CE	Ministries of John the Baptist and Jesus
30	Crucifixion, resurrection, and ascension of Jesus
30	Day of Pentecost, establishment of church
30–31/33	Earliest church in Jerusalem
31–33	Stephen murdered; persecution arises; Gospel promoted throughout Samaria and Galilee; Saul of Tarsus converted, travels to Arabia and back to Damascus
32–35	Founding of church in Antioch
34–36	Paul travels from Damascus to Jerusalem
34/36–38/41	Paul in Cilicia
37–42	Cornelius converted, Antiochenes preach Christ to Gentiles; Barnabas sent to Antioch, goes and gets Paul from Tarsus; after one year, Agabus comes and predicts famine
41–44	Famine predicted by Agabus comes to pass; Antiochenes send aid to Judea to elders by hand of Paul and Barnabas

*Ranges of dates are often given due to lack of specific information in the Bible or other history. The ranges found on this timeline reflect the generally accepted timeframe for the placement of these events.

41–44	Herod Agrippa I executes James the brother of John, imprisons Peter; Peter freed miraculously
44	Death of Herod Agrippa I
44–46	Paul and Barnabas in Antioch
46–48	First Missionary Journey; Paul and Barnabas promote Gospel in Cyprus and southern Asia Minor
48–50	Jerusalem conference
49–50/51	Paul begins Second Missionary Journey with Silas, returns to southern Asia Minor, preaches in Macedonia and Athens
50/51–52	Paul preaches in Corinth for eighteen months; 1 and 2 Thessalonians written
52	Paul brought before Gallio, departs from Corinth
52–53	After quick stop in Ephesus, Paul travels to Antioch; Apollos converted by work of Aquila and Priscilla in Ephesus
54–55	Paul travels through Galatia and Phrygia, returning to Ephesus; Apollos and Peter to Corinth
55–57	Third Missionary Journey: Paul preaches in Ephesus; likely trip to Corinth; Galatians, 1 and 2 Corinthians written
57–58	Riot in Ephesus, Paul imprisoned in Ephesus (?); Paul makes journey again through Macedonia and Achaia, begins trip to Jerusalem; Romans written
58–60	Paul imprisoned in Jerusalem and taken to Caesarea for two years; Colossians, Philemon written
60–62	Paul sent to Rome, under house arrest for two years; Ephesians, Philippians written. Luke probably writes both Luke and Acts at this time.
61	James the brother of the Lord killed in Jerusalem

62–66	Peter writes 1 and 2 Peter from Rome; executed in Rome; Hebrew author writes Hebrews
62–64	Paul travels to Macedonia, Crete, possibly Spain, possibly other places; 1 Timothy and Titus written
64–66	Paul again imprisoned; 2 Timothy written; death of Paul
68–70	Jewish revolt and destruction of Jerusalem; 1 Clement likely written
90–96	John writes 1–3 John and Revelation; end of New Testament revelation
114–115	Ignatius of Antioch writes letters to various churches, suffers martyrdom
115–155	Polycarp of Smyrna writes letter to Philippi, suffers martyrdom

Bibliography

Geographical References

Frank, Harry. *Hammond Atlas of the Bible Lands,* Revised
 Edition. Maplewood, New Jersey: Hammond Incorporated,
 1997 [1977].

Laney, J. Carl. *Concise Bible Atlas.* Peabody, Massachusetts:
 Hendrickson Publishers, Incorporated, 2003 [1988].

Primary Historical Sources

Epiphanius of Salamis. *Of Weights and Measures.*

Eusebius of Caesarea. *History of the Church.* Translated in Schaff
 and Wade, *Nicene and Post-Nicene Fathers,* Volume I, 81–402.

Flavius Josephus. *The Antiquities of the Jews.* Translated in
 Whiston, *The Works of Josephus,* 27–542.

Ignatius of Antioch. *Letter to the Ephesians.* Translated in
 Roberts and Donaldson, *The Ante-Nicene Fathers,* Volume I,
 49–58.

_____. *Letter to the Philadelphians.* Translated in Roberts
 and Donaldson, *The Ante-Nicene Fathers,* Volume I, 79–85.

_____. *Letter to the Romans.* Translated in Roberts and
 Donaldson, *The Ante-Nicene Fathers,* Volume I, 73–78.

_____. *Letter to the Smyrneans.* Translated in Roberts and
 Donaldson, *The Ante-Nicene Fathers,* Volume I, 86–92.

"Ignatius of Antioch." *Letter to the Philippians*. Translated in Roberts and Donaldson, *The Ante-Nicene Fathers*, Volume I, 116–119.

Irenaeus. *Against Heresies*. Translated in Roberts and Donaldson, *The Ante-Nicene Fathers*, Volume I, 315–567.

Polycarp. *Letter to the Philippians*. Translated in Roberts and Donaldson, *The Ante-Nicene Fathers*, Volume I, 31–36.

Suetonius. *The Twelve Caesars*. Translated by Robert Graves. London, England: Penguin Books, 1989 [1957].

Tacitus, Cornelius. *The Annals of Imperial Rome*. Translated by Michael Grant. London, England: Penguin Books, 1989 [1956].

Secondary Historical Sources
Halley, Hampton. *Halley's Bible Handbook*, 25th edition. Grand Rapids, Michigan: Zondervan Publishing House, 2000.

Tenney, Merrill C. *Exploring New Testament Culture*. Iowa Falls, Iowa: World Bible Publishers, Inc., 2000 [1965].

Biblical Resources
Boles, Leo. *A Commentary on the Acts of the Apostles*. Nashville, Tennessee: Gospel Advocate Company, 1989 [1940].

Lipscomb, David. *A Commentary on Second Corinthians and Galatians*. Nashville, Tennessee: Gospel Advocate Company, 1989.

Milligan, Robert. *A Commentary on the Epistle to the Hebrews*. Nashville, Tennessee: Gospel Advocate Company, 1989.